The Fear to

Persevere

A Practitioner's Review Surviving Abuse and Domestic Violence

by Albert Grieve

The Fear to Persevere
A Practitioner's Review Surviving Abuse and Domestic Violence
© 2023 by Albert Grieve

ISBN: 978-1-958117-16-3 (paperback)
ISBN: 978-1-958117-17-0 (eBook)

Library of Congress Control Number: 2023917140

Editor: Melvese Johnson
Cover Illustrator: Claire Joaqin

by *JATNE* PUBLISHING™
South Carolina, US

Table of Contents

Chapter 1

Introduction

(intrə'dəkSHən[1])

"If I could turn back the hands of time,"

I would change nothing.

---

[1] Against wise counseling, I have chosen to retain certain words and phrases that may not be easily recognizable to all education levels because I want to encourage growth and development. I always look up words and concepts with which I am unfamiliar. I will also use footnotes to add context, depth and to point out learning opportunities. I have chosen this format because education is one of the things that helped me gain control of my life and my future.

I would change nothing about my past because of the life I have today. I am married with three amazing children. We live comfortably and my children will never face the hardships I survived. Only after considering the atrocities I endured as a child and the hardships I faced after emancipation will this statement gain mass and clarity. I have suffered from all forms of abuse, experienced a homicide, and survived being a ward of the state (foster care). All I can say through this is, "I am alive." Not all who succumb to the type of environment in which I grew up can say this. My mother did not make it. Too many struggle to get by. While I may have particular wishes—I do not know what it is like to have a mother as an adult, teenager, or "normal"[2] child, for that matter—I am blessed to want nothing. I start here so the message of hope is not lost to anyone surviving abuse, neglect, or domestic violence. In the same vein, this is not an attempt to rail against the authorities charged with protecting the defenseless and investigating these loathsome acts of violence.

On the contrary, the authorities eventually connected the dots. They saw the forest through the trees and removed me from my home, putting me into a safer place. Once I was finally removed[3]

---

[2] Normalcy has always been an elusive concept. Growing up in my home environment and being a state ward (in foster care), I tried to not be different and often struggled to find "normal."

[3] When I speak of removal, I am describing the process where the state takes a child from their home (becoming a legal custodian for the child) and places them in the foster care ("into care") system. There are many variations such as a diversional placement, but my background details ample

2

from that dangerous situation, the years of having to survive enabled me to thrive. Had investigators not deemed my condition warranted removal, there may have been more deaths, and I would not have the present family and life I hold so dear. I am not setting a low bar. As an attorney and former police officer, I know the difficulties in investigating and pursuing child welfare cases and domestic violence. Sadly, while the details of my story are specific to me, the types of things that occurred are not unique, instead occurring with alarming frequency. Agencies are struggling to recruit and retain good staff. Practitioners struggle to work in this field and deal with secondary trauma while giving their families the lives they deserve due to being overworked and undercompensated for their services. Through litigating on behalf of Missouri Children's Division, and training practitioners, I saw far too many cases that reminded me of my childhood—some eerily so. While there have been substantial improvements, I feel there is so much further yet to go.

In furtherance of this goal, I am stepping out of my comfort zone and sharing my story. I did not write this book from start to finish; instead, I tackled topics and experiences as I was mentally able to face them. In sections, I may express a viewpoint that is not healthy, but it was how I felt in the moment as I was processing my trauma. By writing this book, I have recognized that I am on a healing journey and have made substantial

justification warranting our removal from our father's custody. However, the authorities chose instead to let us remain in the home.

progress. However, I have much further to go and recognize the importance of others beginning this process much sooner—hopefully, as a child. So, let the systemic failures that contributed to my worsening home environment serve as lessons for learning everywhere—ones that shock and appall but must be told on behalf of countless silent voices. I share not only my past but the documentation I obtained from authorities dealing with my history to highlight missed opportunities for intervention and learning lessons that practitioners can utilize moving forward.

Sharing my journey has been beneficial but difficult. Since escaping my childhood's maelstrom of chaos and trauma, I have learned that those experiences have not escaped me. When you leave care (state custody), care does not leave you. Exploring the extent of the "what" we are surviving is much more challenging but worth pushing through. Sharing not only aids me, but others may be able to beneficially see their trauma from a different perspective or with increased clarity. Whenever I speak publicly about my background, people approach me afterwards to acknowledge shared experiences. They often are unable to or are uncomfortable sharing their specific incidents, but they express comfort knowing they are not alone. We are making it through. We are surviving. Emphasis on present tense. Ultimately, my goal is to enable prevention and earlier intervention so others do not have to be in survivor mode.

Through sharing in training and speaking events, I have become very mindful that merely telling my story has the potential to be traumatizing. I know it is hard to read in written form, but it is harder to write and share, even harder to have lived through, and to live with is the hardest of all. I maintain it is difficult as an outsider to go beyond possessing sympathy into genuinely understanding in a way that moves them into a different form of action. I do not wish my childhood on anyone, but I know there is a benefit in palpably sharing my experiences. It is priceless when a practitioner can see something through my story that makes them better equipped to deal with complex cases of abuse, neglect, and domestic violence; potentially, seeing a case they are working on in a different light or perspective. I share my story with brutal honesty because I believe certain things in this world cannot be fully grasped without experience. A palpable training, and hopefully this book, can be the next closest thing.

It is difficult to understand my current station in life without knowing where I am from and what I endured. Only then can the gravity of the following take hold: waking up, owning my own home and not being incarcerated or on drugs are all significant accomplishments. What exactly did I endure?

First, a disclaimer is in order. It is okay if anyone reading this needs to exercise self-care because the experiences I share may cause someone to relive or recall an experience they or someone they know may have gone through. There is nothing wrong with mental self-care. In fact, if mental health was more of a priority in our society, much of my childhood experiences may not have ever happened.

The following chapters will provide greater detail about my experiences and the resulting impact. There are instances where I speak primarily as a practitioner and other areas where I can only describe something from my perspective as a child.

Concisely, all of my trauma stems from the actions of my father and things my mother was forced to do because of him. As the middle child of three, I also witnessed horrible acts against my two sisters. My father is an angry and abusive alcoholic.[4] I often did not attend school on time because I was always healing from some injury. When I started school after a break or vacation, the wounds often had not healed enough to prevent teachers or authorities from taking notice. Concerned individuals called our home, and subsequently, we had frequent visits from the authorities. The authorities failed to thoroughly investigate and review the entirety of our history or interactions with other agencies. A convincing superficial lie was generally enough to alleviate their concerns, preventing our removal from this environment.

While the story of my siblings is one for them to share, parts are inextricably intertwined with mine.

---

[4] Eventually, my father was prosecuted for sexual abuse committed against my older sister. Even after being released from parole post-incarceration, it appears alcohol still brings out the anger and aggression inside of him. Throughout his term of parole, I held a lingering hope that maybe, just maybe, there had been a change. That hope was misplaced.

My older sister Claire's story would eventually lead to our removal from the situation. My mother, who was African-American, tried to run away numerous times.[5] She would often be placed in a mental institution as my convincing articulate Caucasian father would parade her medications in front of law enforcement, proclaiming she was crazy. My mother thought my father was going to kill her. Each time she was institutionalized, the doctors would change and adjust her medications, keeping her hospitalized until she recanted. While she was away, there were other forms of abuse occurring. I can never "un-hear" the sounds of my father having sex with my older sister in our bedroom and the quiet cries of my sister giving up hope.

As this cycle continued, my father learned and refined his methodology according to each interaction with the authorities. The violence got perpetually worse, not even culminating when my mother died at the hands of my father. At the age of thirteen, I learned what rigor mortis was as my mother was carried out of our apartment by the fire department; her clothes soiled, her face painted in dried blood. Her body frozen in a hogtied position (with her arms and feet stuck behind her back).

---

[5] On occasion, she would go to an emergency shelter. I recall going with her once. It was kind of a hidden location, surrounded by a cyclone fence topped with horizontal barbed wire strands. We were given a bunk, some blankets, and minimal hygiene supplies. My mother wanted me to guard our stuff. Although the staff and some of the people were nice, most inhabitants seemed menacing and destitute. It was a scary place for a child.

7

Despite this homicide,[6] and after multiple reports and allegations of sexual abuse occurring in the home, my siblings and I went to school the following Monday.

<u>Cordova High School, Cindy Evans, Counselor</u>: "Ms. Evans reported she had talked to CLAIRE YOUNG on a number of occasions. She stated CLAIRE has very good grades and a very good attendance record. She reported she saw no red flags with this family until after the mother had died. Ms. Evans stated CLAIRE came to school the Monday after her mother died and did not tell anyone about the death of her mother..." (Source: California Department of Health and Human Services, Child Protective Services)

Despite the concerns of my father, we did not come into care that week. Days became weeks, and weeks became months, and I was nearing the limit of hope as the abuse I suffered took a turn for the perverse (harm that has had a more significant

---

[6] No criminal charges have been brought, nor will they appear to be brought after speaking to a Sacramento County Sheriff Detective in late 2020. I'll discuss this more in-depth later, but criminal charges would change nothing about the past.

negative impact on me than all the physical abuse I suffered combined).

4 her mother dying the day before. ASHLEY was found outside the classroom after school crying and
5 told her teacher her mother had died. The teacher then took her to the principal and the principal
6 took ASHLEY home. When the principal and ASHLEY got to the home, the father appeared to be
7 very "hyper." He showed the principal the kitchen cupboards that were full of food, and showed Ms.
8 Kerekes his carpenter license to show that he was licensed as a carpenter. She reported he appeared
9 to be very concerned that Children's Protective Services would be called and take the children, so he
was showing the principal how organized and well he was caring for the children.

"...ASHLEY was found outside the classroom after school crying and told her teacher her mother had died. The teacher then took her to the principal and the principal took ASHLEY home. When the principal and ASHLEY got to the home, the father appeared to be very 'hyper.' He showed the principal the kitchen cupboards that were full of food and showed Ms. Kerekes his carpenter license to show that he was licensed as a carpenter. She reported he appeared to be very concerned that Children's Protective Services would be called and take the children, so he was showing the principal how organized and well he was caring for the children." (Source: California Department of Health and Human Services, Child Protective Services)

I long doubted the ability of any agency or individual to save my siblings and I, but this was a whole new level of horror. My father had just killed my mother, and we went to school as if everything was normal. Sure, the vice principal at my middle school indicated he had concerns and would keep

9

a closer eye on me, but that did nothing to stop what was happening behind closed doors at home.

10

11   Mr. Willeford reported ALBERT appeared to be immature socially. He stated ALBERT would

12 go from one extreme to another. He noted ALBERT would be very friendly at one moment and then

13 very angry the next. He reported ALBERT had been sent to the counselor on seven different

14 occasions for discipline. The last referral was for the sexual comment regarding "dildo stuck up her

15 ass" which was a red flag to the school that there may be some sexual abuse issues in the home.

16 There was no follow up on this comment. Mr. Willeford reported he wondered about possible

sexual abuse and would pay closer attention to ALBERT and his behavior.

"Mr. Willeford reported ALBERT appeared to be immature socially. He stated ALBERT would go from one extreme to another. He noted ALBERT would be very friendly at one moment and then very angry the next. He reported ALBERT has been sent to the counselor on seven different occasions for discipline. The last referral was for the sexual comment regarding 'dildo stuck up her ass' which was a red flag to the school that there may be some sexual abuse issues in the home. There was no follow up on this comment. Mr. Willeford reported he wondered about possible sexual abuse and would pay closer attention to ALBERT and his behavior." (Source: California Department of Health and Human Services, Child Protective Services)

Damage was done that could never be erased; the lingering effects of most of these hardships are still being felt today. Why was I too weak to protect myself? Why didn't I have the courage to stand up to my father? Is it not my job to protect my sisters, and what about my mother? There was still a part of me left inside…but not for long. How could I live with myself as a child? I could have done something—anything. At a heavy price, Claire stepped up and tried to kill my father. She failed. She then tried to kill herself. Not long after, my sisters and I came into care (state custody) but were forever separated. That, too, has had lasting consequences.

While I was grateful that I came into foster care as things improved in some obvious ways, they worsened in others. I would still change nothing about my life. Serving in law enforcement is a privilege not all can experience. I am a licensed attorney in child welfare. I am blessed to have an amazing wife and three fantastic boys. My most outstanding achievement will always be the life I am giving my children. My oldest is stellar academically and nationally ranked in athletics. My middle child is great in school and nationally ranked in track and field. My youngest has nothing but possibilities ahead of him (but as of this writing has a love for track as well). To trade my past would be to lose my present family, which I cannot do. I have come to appreciate that all things get smaller in the rearview mirror (it just does not mean they are gone).

As I share my journey, the documentation included was obtained from Child Protective Services (CPS) (through a records request of my juvenile file from California Department of Health and Human Services, Child Protective Services). Even Department of Justice record excerpts are copies that had been obtained by CPS and included in my file.[7] It was a very stressful (spanning 18 months) and time-consuming process to obtain these records, and I had to pay for them, so I did not seek documentation from other agencies. However, I succeeded in obtaining things like my immunization records, grade cards, and photos of myself, in addition to court and investigatory documentation.

In all fairness, much of the exhaustive summary documentation I will cite, including the example below, was generated months after my mother's homicide. While I am reviewing the files with hindsight, it demonstrates there was information that *could have been obtained* well in advance. When training, I highlight the importance of identifying *and contacting* as many collateral contacts as possible while viewing a lack of a child's social connections as a warning sign of isolation requiring closer scrutiny. Consider what information was available in my community that led to the following documented rumors and statements (read lines 15-18/the underlined text carefully).

---

[7] In Missouri, unsubstantiated Children's Division records are not retained indefinitely, but hopefully contemporaneous records were kept by responding law enforcement which can be utilized in subsequent investigations. In my case, Child Protective Services records were kept and law records appear to have been destroyed. Redundancy is important.

"...Mrs. Palmer reported the situation was very odd. She reported CLAIRE had gotten paint on the wall when they were decorating a Christmas tree. CLAIRE and Ms. Grieve appeared very fearful and stated they needed to have the paint. Mr. and Mrs. Palmer reported they did not doubt that the father was involved in the death of her mother. They reported she was 'so afraid' of him that they think that she was afraid that he could have killed her. They have heard rumors around the apartment complex, 'He finally did it. He finally killed her.' It was reported by the managers that Mr. Grieve drinks all of the time and at one time, he threatened some of his neighbors and said, 'I got a gun. I'm going to shoot ever nigger in this complex. I've got a gun.'" (Source: California Department of Health and Human Services, Child Protective Services)

Additionally, once a person is removed from this type of situation, a whole new battle begins relating to processing what has happened and trying to find a way forward (a way to heal the scars of trauma). I am still engaged in that battle but have won numerous victories by digging deep into my trauma, writing this book, and expelling some of the toxicity (feel to heal). I reached this point with the help of countless others. If it takes a village to raise a child, what does it take to raise and nurture a child exposed to this kind of abuse and neglect? Ideally, more than a village, but it starts with you and me making noise and increasing awareness, even if it is something as simple as a social media post to show others what matters the most.

Chapter 2

Cannot Forget

(ka͵nät fər'get)

"You shall not pass!" –Lord of the Rings

I must dispel any notion that I am a strong and courageous person for sharing my journey. It is difficult to go from the life I am living right now to the dark maelstrom of trauma that was my childhood. Months can go by when I remember nothing from my childhood. No memories surface; I do not dwell on the loss of my mother, and vivid images from the past do not haunt me. These are the good months. From time to time, however, a scent, a sound, or something I see will cause me to remember something from the past. My middle son, Kai, was playing a video game with his friends when he said, "If I go down, we all go down." My younger sister, Ashley, made a similar statement to the authorities concerning my father (see excerpt in Chapter 8). It is not always so directly parallel. The strangest things sometimes will lead me down the dark path of memory lane.

Hot water sometimes reminds me of my mother. She took quite a bit of medication for various things with which she had been diagnosed (rightly or wrongly) and always liked to drink hot water. Most people I know prefer cold water, perhaps with ice. I gave her hot water, just as she wanted, on the last day I saw her alive. I fight tears from welling up in my eyes because I cannot forget failing to tell her I love her on that day. As I write this, I am thirty-seven years old. That day, she was also thirty-seven. I did not know it would be the day my father would kill her.

As I recall little events, I pick up speed and travel faster, remembering more significant events and winding further along a sorrowful one-way stretch of highway leading only to despair and guilt. One memory leads to the next, and I cannot exit. Before I can prevent it, I am overcome by the imagery of terror and regret. It is like a storm is brewing in my mind, the visibility of my present is reducing, and I still cannot slow down. Terror from the unknown such as "will I make it through the night?" or "how bad will it be?" are present and my life almost becomes surreal. I lose contact with the ground, and it feels as if the storm is pulling me into its eye. I regret my lack of willpower to run away or put a stop to things. Deafening noise[8] creates sensory overload. Do I have the strength to end it? It is hard to escape from reliving my past and descend back to the ground. There is nothing to grasp; the now possesses no meaning. The past becomes an all-consuming horror vortex that destroys all it contacts.

I try to rationalize the past (and acts for which I carry guilt) by reminding myself I was just a child. Somehow, that thought provides little comfort. As I grow older, I see and hear stories of the heroic acts of others in seeking help, escaping from their situations, or facing them head-on by physically confronting their abusers. Sometimes people fail, but sometimes they are triumphant. I tell myself I was a little runt as a child. What chance did I have to fight my ex-military father? I thought about trying to hurt him with a weapon while he was

---

[8] I liken trauma to tinnitus in that only the one suffering experiences the symptoms; nobody else can perceive the manifestations. Tinnitus is characterized by hearing a sound when no external sound is present, and it typically takes the form of a ringing or buzzing in the ears. Tinnitus can be so deafening and overwhelming that those experiencing it cannot function, not unlike trauma.

sleeping, but I could never bring myself to act on those thoughts.

I attempt to force it all out, bury it, and find something to occupy my mind. I do all I can to encapsulate my past in a chest, lock it tight, and bring a building down on it. I know it will resurface again, but I try to buy some time. Distractions help, things to keep me grounded in the present moment such as playing games with my children. These "footings" tether me to the ground and keep me from being swept away by dark memories. The storm clears and the past loses control over me for now.

Considering this struggle, it is beyond counterintuitive to intentionally place myself into my past to disclose what I am overcoming. I've always wanted to make good come from my past, and if sharing provides my audience with tools or insight to prevent others from going through what I did, then it is worth it. I share because I am blessed to be able to do so, and I feel blessed because I share.

While we all know that disclosing a traumatic event is a process, I have realized that healing is also a process. Each time I disclose, I learn that my world does not collapse. Every time I share, I get more comfortable providing additional information and feel more capable of quieting the storm.

This journey started with fear and anxiety but has led me to understand that I have no hate in my heart. At age thirty-six, I reached out to my paroled father in preparation for some conference presentations. I had no idea where the experience would lead. Would I curse at him? Could courage permit me to ask tough questions? Will panic overrun me?

I learned that as a grown man with prior law enforcement experience, I was utterly frightened. The thought of talking to him and hearing his voice transported me back to my childhood. I had physical manifestations of fear; my heart was racing, and I was sweating at the thought of interacting with him. But why? I was thousands of miles away. Why wasn't I in control? I did not want to do this. I told myself I did not need to do this, but I felt compelled to make a perfect presentation.

I had no expectations, but I was looking for something. Maybe, just maybe, my father would give me something valuable, some epiphany, some insight into the mind of an abuser that would create an "aha" moment for practitioners. I could find more purpose in the harm I suffered. I approached the conversation from a practitioner's perspective, not that of a son speaking to a father—I was not ready to speak to him as his child. What would I call him? I do not view a "father" as having a relationship with their children. Instead, "father" is a designation attributed to a person on The Maury Show. I use "dad" with my children. Focus, be on guard, I commanded myself.

We talked and the world kept turning. No physical harm happened to me. We had numerous conversations about superficial things, such as the weather. With each talk, I gained more courage to start asking questions in search of helpful insights for investigators. I saw no point in asking about our past in terms of, "why did you do this?" I felt nothing would, or could, change.

During one of our conversations, I finally began disclosing where I was in my life. I had mentioned that I was an attorney, and he replied that he knew I was smart, figuring I might graduate valedictorian one day. After several minutes of meaningless conversation, I informed him that I had graduated valedictorian from a university. Was I seeking his approval? Who wouldn't want positive acknowledgment from their parents? During another conversation, he said something funny, but I fought the urge to laugh. Could the fact that I laughed at something he said signal that I condoned all the things that happened during our childhood? Should I let down my guard? I wanted to...but why?

One conversation I had with my father drifted to the topic of cooking. He said something about me likely being a good cook, and I acknowledged the diversity in my cooking talents, but then I grew quiet. I recalled all the times I was repeatedly beaten when he would stand over me, forcing me to cook ramen on a stovetop, beating me more each time I got it wrong. I must have been seven or eight years old, and it is hard enough to do something when a person is standing over your shoulder, watching your every move. A whole new level exists when that person physically beats you when your efforts fail to meet their standards. I would have to cook ramen again and again, causing it to boil over, or cooking it too long or not long enough. Each failure brought more wasted food, food our family needed because we were poor. Nevertheless, again and again, I would get it wrong; my mistakes brought beatings worse than the last. I was done talking to my father for the day.

Eventually, I obtained enough conversations to use in my presentation. I had a few quotes, but they were not what I expected. There was one conversation where I stated my father killed my mother. He heard me and responded but did not dispute what I said. I assume I was looking for validation, more proof that I did not imagine things. Still, nothing changed. But the most significant takeaway was realizing my father was no longer the monster I knew as a child in that I am not afraid of him. When I found him on the sex offender registry, I first noticed his height and weight. I was bigger than he was. Shortly after starting to talk to him, he informed me that he had had cancer, but it was in remission. I did not even know what to do with that information.

During our conversations, I started to understand my father was not as clever as I thought. He merely got away with telling superficial lies to investigators because there was inadequate or no follow-up. He still did horrible things and was very manipulative, just not as bright as I thought.

After preparing for my conferences, weeks would go by when I would not reach out or respond to his communications. I might send a text message or talk briefly on the phone, and we would discuss the weather or an unoffending topic. I had nothing further to gain by talking to him, so I had no desire to reach out or respond. Then one day, I received a text message from him, essentially saying I needed to respond because he was going to die when he learned his cancer had returned. I ignored his request. When I was a teenager, he had also sent me letters from prison demanding that I respond to his communications with the not-so-subtle suggestions that he would otherwise commit suicide (see the images at the end of this chapter). While I did not respond to his cancer text directly, I did inform my younger sister, who spoke with him more often than I did.

The last update I received on my father was that he was no longer on parole. My younger sister reached out to the manager where he was staying because she had not heard from him for a while. The manager told her that he had gotten drunk one night and was blasting music. He got into an altercation with one of the other residents and subsequently fled. I have no idea where he is or what he is doing. Neither my younger sister nor I have had contact with him in any way. At least for now, he has gone from my life again. I can deal with this. For many years, while incarcerated, he was dead to me, like actually deceased. One of the most emotional times in my life was when I learned he had come back to life in the form of being released from prison. Atrocious notification from the state aside, I did not know where to begin processing this information. So, I am okay with going back to him being deceased. I am glad I maintained my guardrails and did not get my hopes up riding this emotional rollercoaster. While I am still broken and not okay, I feel I am in the best place I have ever been dealing with my past and all that comes with it. I only wish I had my present perspective as a child.

As a youth, I was uncomfortable sharing my background because I believed the recipient could not handle the truth. Therefore, I was only willing to disclose that which would produce a quantity of judgment and drama I was ready to tolerate. I felt it was important not to upset their happy little world, not realizing I was harming myself. Beyond some skeletal disclosure, I kept everything else locked up in a chest. It was enough that I had to deal with everything I endured without piling on judgment, pity, or other unwelcome responses from some people finding out about my childhood. But if I can face my abuser and everything entailed yet be alright, I feel I'm ready to memorialize my disclosure for the greater good forever. I am prepared to enter the trauma storm because I know how to protect myself. The best place to start is the beginning.

☺

If by chance either Familiesfirst or your social worker has stopped you from writing to me because of my mentioning the quarter package thing in my letters to you it's not fare. And you should at least be allowed t write me one last letter explaining to me that you are no longer allowed to write me if in fact this is what's wrong! Or if its you and you no longer wish to write me, pleas just write and let me know this Albert.

If I dont hear from you soon then I'll jus have to assume that its all over between you and me! And then I shall just give up son because without regular letters from you I do not wish to go on any longer. I will ha no reason to live any longer, only reason I hanging in at all is because of your letters. I give me hope and a reason to live. So please, please, please write to me as soon as possible. I am just waiting to hear from you, please write

P.S. Please say hello to Ashley and Claire for me. When is Claire going to write?

Please take care now Albert, I hope to hear from you soon!

Love Dad

(Source: California Department of Health and Human Services, Child Protective Services)

Chapter 3

Early Days

(ərlē dās)

"Once upon a time," things were not as violent or perverse...

My early memories are somewhat disjointed. Some periods are entirely blanked out, but others are vivid. One memory often leads to another that may seem unrelated to others. While child disclosures, especially younger children, do not follow neat chronological patterns, I have always struggled with linear thought. Law school was particularly challenging in this regard. Instead of A B C, my mind follows a pattern of A 3 Squirrel. Lastly, there are some things that I cannot explain except through my childhood perspective.

Not everything in my childhood was horrendous. Not everything my father did had a negative impact. Things were not always so toxic. I try to portray both the positive and negative as I share my story. There are lessons to be learned through it all.

In the same way, a practitioner or investigator should tell all sides of a case in which they are involved. All too often, I saw practitioners in court only sharing adverse facts and getting characterized by the defense as biased. Do not allow the defense in a court of law to paint a picture of cherry-picking facts or coloring the truth—there should be no distractions from the points we are trying to prove and the lives we are trying to save. So, freely share that the defendant, suspect, or alleged perpetrator volunteers at a soup kitchen and then describe the allegations of molestation. It is a beautiful occasion when the judge stops a defense from grandstanding to say, "We covered that, counselor; move on."

*　　　　　*　　　　　*

I was born at UC Davis Medical Center in Sacramento, CA. As the middle child of a sibling group of three, I had one older and one younger sister. Claire and I share the same mom, but she had a different father. Ashley and I had the same parents.

My father was from Seattle, WA. He met my mother in Sacramento. Early in his relationship with her, he worked as a journeyman carpenter. I have our family photo album which contains a brochure from Continental Store Fixtures where he used to work. My father was very proud of his work. He had picked up some construction skills in the military from being part of the Navy Seabees stationed in Anchorage, AK. They were a unit that specialized in constructing buildings and forward bases.

I do not recall my mother ever working; she was on disability, SSA and SSI. As far as I know, she had always been on disability while with my father. She had been diagnosed with depression which was later changed to paranoid schizophrenia. As I got older, this diagnosis would be weaponized often against her. She was believed to be delusional because she thought her husband was trying to hurt her children and kill her. She was heavily medicated due to her "beliefs."

Growing up, I did not know much about my extended family. I know that my mother's family was from the Los Angeles area, and as a teenager in the foster care system, I would eventually meet one of her relatives.[9] I also connected with others through social media as an adult. Through this contact, I learned my mother had an extremely traumatic childhood and was victimized as a youth.

As for my father, I overheard conversations that he had, such as one about his grandfather who worked on the Seattle Space Needle. Supposedly, just before the opening day, my father's grandfather had been tasked with ensuring everything was working properly, and the Space Needle failed to rotate correctly. I also remember him talking about having two children through a previous relationship, but I never verified that. Claire recalls him speaking often about these other kids. He denied it when we spoke after his release from prison.

My earliest memory is playing in a small blue wading pool in front of our house, although now it's more of a recollection of a memory. I was maybe three years old, and we had a place with horizontal white siding and blue shutters on either side of the front windows. My father always liked to play music loud. On this day, he played a song I later identified as Songbird by Kenny G. I do not have many fond

---

[9] I had no known relatives until I was sixteen years old. At that point, I was comfortable with my school and foster home, and the agency I was with tried to place me with an elderly aunt I had never met. I was forced to do a weeklong visit with her. I spent the entire visit in misery from being allergic to her countless cats. It did not help that when we first met, I tried to show off my wrestling strength by lifting her off the ground when I hugged her. I heard and felt the cracks in her back as I lifted her, and I think she had to seek treatment. She was very nice, but ultimately it was not a good fit.

memories of my childhood, except this is one that has stuck with me. When I got married at age twenty, I played Songbird at our wedding. Well, I guess more accurately, my wife allowed me to play the song in the venue we were going to be married in, but well before any of the proceedings began. I held on to this memory because, looking back, it was unusual that things were joyous and so far from chaotic.

When I was too young for school, my older sister had a parent-teacher meeting at a nearby elementary school, and I was brought along. I stole a toy from the classroom and brought it home with me. It was discovered I had taken this toy. I was disciplined, then brought back to the school to return the toy. I was not a perfect child. My older sister told me I was a handful as a kid. I was hyper and always getting into stuff.

When I began attending kindergarten at Pacific Elementary School, conditions were beginning to deteriorate. We were no longer in the house, and my father would tell people he left work to care for us kids. He claimed my mother could not care for us due to her mental health. This necessarily meant we had less money, and with a decrease in income came an increase in stress and alcohol consumption. Around this time, we were staying at Greystone Apartments off 41st Ave near Franklin Blvd. The sprawling nearby industrial complex used to be a Campbell's Soup factory. It seemed like the smell of food went on for miles.

I used to walk to school, east on 41st Street, past Rainbow Park off of Martin Luther King Jr. Blvd. I wished I could play more at that park, but we had to go straight to school and back home. I was so mad at my older sister one day because I had to walk to school with her, and she decided to go to a friend's house. She was not supposed to. I complained that I would not make it to breakfast, and she gave me some lemon grass growing in front of the house—lemon grass! I did not make it to breakfast that day and was so hungry. I did not always get to eat dinner.

Based on our finances, we ate breakfast and lunch through the free lunch program at school. Oftentimes, this was the only place I could really eat. As I got older, I became more accustomed to dealing with the headaches that come from starving. I often would skip lunch, so I had more time to play. Had I not missed so many meals, I may look even more like the Rock[10] than I do today.

We also had food stamps when they came in books, long before the EBT card. At the beginning of each month, my father would make out a long list of all the groceries we needed for the month and then take stuff off that list so he could sell some of the food stamps for cash, usually $0.50 on the dollar. That cash was mostly used to buy beer, wine, and brandy. We were a family of five with too many resources allocated for alcohol. So, what we had did not go a long way.

We were poor and it showed. I did not mind store brand clothes and shoes from Payless Shoe Store. I just hated that the clothes were always two

---

[10] I had someone tell me I looked like the Rock when I was a cop, but I think they just did not want to get a ticket.

sizes too small. We generally walked or took the bus to go shopping. There were times when we had our own transportation, but it was inconsistent or went away altogether as I got older. I remember sitting on the floorboard of a vehicle while my father was in the blood bank, and getting into trouble when I did not keep my head down. We didn't keep that vehicle.

I recall later, my father was drinking and blasting music. I do not know what my mother was doing. I was giving my younger sister a ride on my back as I crawled on my hands and knees. She kept cutting my hair with scissors, and I tried to tell her to stop. I raised my hand to stop her, and she nearly cut off my right ring finger. A neighbor drove me to the hospital in a cool old "Bomb" car, because I assume we did not have transportation at that time.

When we moved to our next apartment, we had a different car at some point because I remember the violence connected to it. The only time I remember police arresting my father was after a violent episode before Christmas. A lot of stuff got broken and the Christmas tree was knocked[11] over. We had to get a neighbor to break the steering column on our four-door sedan and bond my father out. He was back home that night. This was the same month and vehicle in which he was stabbing me with a screwdriver; more on that later.

On occasion we would walk to the grocery store and might use a cab to help us bring the groceries

---

[11] Maybe this is when my father learned to hide the damage that was caused.

home. Other times, we had to walk back from the grocery store carrying everything, which usually was too much for us to handle—evidenced when bags would break. While still in elementary school, I vividly recall being disciplined for crying because the bags hurt my hands. Those plastic handles got smaller and smaller, carrying weight over time. This was not abuse—just poverty.

Generally, we would go to the food closet after the middle of the month and carry those groceries back too. I remember we would get government USDA food like peanut butter or powdered milk. They tried to give us various ingredients, perishable goods, and even some dessert-like items. Unfortunately, dessert was something I often did not get. Again, not abuse, but something that sucks if you're a kid.

My father knew how to cook and prided himself on his abilities. The family photo album has certificates my parents received for a cooking and nutrition class they took. He also was good at baking. He used to follow a USDA recipe for bread, making something like what you would see on an old western TV show. He also, occasionally, baked cinnamon rolls entirely from scratch—the dough and everything, not that stuff you get in a Pillsbury container. When I was a little older but still in elementary school, I remember he used an ABS pipe as a rolling pin when baking. I remember that pipe because it always made a funny sound when he hit me on the head. There was a sound both when he was swinging it in the air and when it cracked me on the skull (like a hollow dull thud). I still have a dent in the rear right corner of my skull that I think was caused when he hit me with the edge of it once.

To cook specific meals, I often got sent to the grocery store to get a handful of items, maybe a bag of groceries or two. I would have to ride the bus and often I was provided some spare change to make a phone call from a payphone. It never failed that every time I went to the store, something I was supposed to buy was not there, was not the right amount, or cost too much. I always got punished for doing wrong and squandering our limited resources.

My father contributed to our limited resources by using cash to purchase alcohol at the beginning of the month. The first few days when we had money, things were not necessarily violent, but they were chaotic (like when my sister cut my finger with scissors). In that chaos, my siblings and I may inevitably do something we were not supposed to and would get in trouble. My father would drink beverages like E&J Brandy, but as his funds got depleted, he switched to King Cobra beer. He also drank a lot of box wine. As the month progressed, he became more violent until he ran out of alcohol. Toward the end of each month, it seemed like he may not have been so horrible when sober, but the bad memories easily displace the good.

I do not feel like I gave my father a reason to be so violent. I was not a bad kid in school, but I know I was hyper and frequently reprimanded for talking out of turn. In my defense, I often knew the answer and the teacher was not calling on me. I recall, in the second grade, I entered a book competition. I wrote and illustrated a book titled *The Bouncing World*. It was planet Earth with arms and legs who did things like going to the grocery store. I remember spending a lot of time drawing the frozen food aisle and detailing things behind the glass doors. I do not recall what the story was about, but toward the end, he started bouncing. He bounced so hard that he shattered into a million pieces. I ended it by saying, "You may believe it or not" (because we used to watch *Ripley's Believe It or Not* a lot). I won second place and was proud of that and the positive feedback I received from school. My father ripped up the book and threw it away with the award. It was as if he wanted to quiet the acclaim I was receiving and did not want me feeling as though I was capable of achievement.

I entered a third-grade science competition and created a solar power oven. I remember I had to scavenge for supplies around my school because I could not get any from home. It was a simple Styrofoam container lined with aluminum foil and covered with Saran wrap. One of the judges put an egg inside the oven and cooked it under the open sun. I won third place. My project and the award were destroyed and thrown away by my father.

I don't look back and mourn the loss of my achievements. I even feel silly sharing this because I have accomplished more significant things in my life like having a license to practice law, but these are important events to explore because they were the first steps towards an awful progression of abuse. I soon grasped that anything I did that was good was taken away from me, and all that was left was bad. I even recall reading a book about diesel trucks and explaining why truckers preferred cab over engine designs (based on the book I had just read with my mother). My father took the book away and argued I was incorrect. I could not even keep the moment when my mother was proud of me.

My father did not just take away, he gave me things too. When I was in first or second grade, he gave me a jalapeno pepper and told me it was a pickle and to bite it. I knew what it was and, at first, declined. He threatened to spank me unless I took a big bite. I complied, and my discomfort brought him great joy. He also made me drink beer and coffee.

It was around this time that we moved from Greystone Apartments to what was then called Greenpoint Apartments. The name was later changed to Summerset Apartments. When I last checked, the apartment complex was still there, right off Martin Luther King Jr. Blvd. From a satellite view, we were in the building just off the southeast corner of the pool. Without looking at a map, I would not have even remembered there was a pool because we never got to use it. We were rarely allowed to socialize with anyone in the building or complex. There were four units in our building. Facing east, looking at our front door, we were in the lower-right apartment. So much violence happened in this tiny place. This is where I received some of the worst beatings.

Chapter 4

Punishments That Show

(ˈpəniSHm(ə)nt T͟Hat SHō)

"Sticks and stones may break your bones, but"
where can you really hide?

Physical abuse does not affect me as much; it does not have the same psychological impact as an adult. At least, so I tell myself. Nevertheless, it still hurt and shaped who I would become. I often missed school days after a break or started the school year late because I had visible injuries. It seemed nothing I could do was right, and I was always finding a way to attract punishments. I was apparently incapable of learning, so my discipline would become more and more extreme. I wanted to learn, to stop the punishments; I simply did not know what I was supposed to be learning.

What was I doing wrong? If I were to sum up all of my experiences, I believe the biggest problem for my father was my existence. I was too skinny, too sick, and my eyes were too big. I got into trouble for saying, "I'm sorry," and how I said, "I'm sorry." I started saying, "I apologize," but that was not good enough either. The way I said it still angered him. When it came to meals, he did not like when I asked, "Can I have some more, please?" Everything angered him. Why could I not get things right? He even made it clear to the authorities that he did not want me.

On 2/7/97, ▓▓▓▓▓▓▓▓▓ to say that Albert was suspended the day before, Mr. Grieve called the reporter "a bitch" and "threw up his hands, didn't want him anymore." The next day Albert had a black eye. CPS investigation unfounded, minor again denied abuse.

"On 2/7/97...to say that Albert was suspended the day before, Mr. Grieve called the reporter 'a bitch' and 'threw up his hands, didn't want him anymore.' The next day Albert had a black eye. CPS investigation unfounded, minor again denied abuse." (Source: California Department of Health and Human Services, Child Protective Services)

I always came up short. Besides my existence or not knowing how to cook Ramen properly, I could never clean well enough. My shortcomings were met swiftly with discipline.

7 alcohol and begin to drink. Sometimes when his father "got drunk", his father was "very scary" and
8 would be "violent". ALBERT reported when he did not do his chores "correctly", his father would
  make him re-do the chore. ALBERT described that "I am the sloppy one of the family", yet the
9 undersigned observed a very neat and meticulous child who was concerned about dirt on his shoe
10 during the interview. ALBERT reported when his father got drunk, his personality would change.
11 He added when his father got drunk, he could be very "mean". ALBERT describes that his father
12 gave him 10 to 14 black eyes by punching him in the eye. ALBERT at first said he got 14 black
13 eyes by his father, and then said, "Well no, maybe 10." ALBERT reported sometimes his father
14 would wake him up, get him out of bed, and start yelling at him and punch him and slug him in the
15 eye.

"...Sometimes when his father 'got drunk', his father was 'very scary' and would be 'violent'. ALBERT reported when he did not do his chores 'correctly', his father would make him re-do the chore. ALBERT described that 'I am the sloppy one of the family', yet the undersigned observed a very neat and meticulous child who was concerned about dirt on his shoe during the interview. ALBERT reported when his father got drunk, his personality would change. He added when his father got drunk, he could be very 'mean'. ALBERT describes that his father gave him 10 to 14 black eyes by punching him in the eye. ALBERT at first said he got 14 black eyes by his father, and then said, 'Well no, maybe 10.' ALBERT reported sometimes his father would wake him up, get him out of bed, and start yelling at him and punch him and slug him in the eye." (Source: California Department of Health and Human Services, Child Protective Services)

I was afraid to go to bed and afraid to wake up. Afraid to sleep because I could not guard against attack, like my father yanking me by my ankle from the top of the bunkbed while I was sleeping, allowing me to fall to the ground. Afraid to wake up and anger him with my presence.

I think the biggest takeaway here for practitioners would be checking assumptions. Generally, we associate neglect, in particular, with unsanitary living conditions. Since my living conditions appeared hyper-sanitary, the assumption was there must not be neglect and that made abuse seem less likely. In other words, our immaculate living conditions were viewed as "the children are being cared for." Then there was a leap in logic that "cared-for children cannot be abused." It was almost as if the alcohol was overlooked because everything else "appeared" okay.

Appearances were deceiving. My father would much later be diagnosed with obsessive-compulsive disorder (OCD)[12] and other things.

---

[12] None of it, in my humble opinion, explained or excused the sexual abuse. Even if I can look past all the physical abuse and deal with it, there is no processing the sexual abuse. It's like when a computer locks up and is not responding. The only thing I can do is power down and restart, but every time I click on the file, it reacts like a virus, and my computer locks up. To compound issues, you cannot call IT, there is no support, and you cannot discuss it with anybody.

Nothing was ever good enough or clean enough, and our failure to do "enough" would violently anger him when he was intoxicated. His frequent intoxication meant we would always face intense discipline for failing to meet unattainable standards. Even in falling short of his OCD ways, the house was very organized, clean, and tidy. My siblings and I were neat and clean—a situation viewed as positive by investigators. We, in turn, felt we were to blame for our ineptitude and invited the consequences if we dare speak up or spoke out regarding what was happening behind closed doors.

10 ASHLEY reported to the undersigned that when her father drank alcohol, she would sometimes
11 get afraid because he would act mad. When first asked if there was physical abuse in the home
12 ASHLEY stated, "My father would not hurt anyone, well maybe the cat." When asked about if he
13 hurt the cat she responded that he sometimes kicked the cat. She reported that her father gave her
14 brother, ALBERT, seven or eight black eyes, he would slug her brother in the eye. ASHLEY
15 reported she remembers her sister, CLAIRE, having one or two blacks eyes the father gave CLAIRE
16 when he was mad at her. ASHLEY reported she did not receive any black eyes and she usually did
17 not get in trouble with her father. ASHLEY reported for some reason her father took out most of his
18 anger on ALBERT. She stated ALBERT would "sass" her father back and her father would get
19 madder and madder at him. ASHLEY reported ALBERT "kinda deserved" getting hit by her father
20 because he would ask silly things like wanting to call his counselor at school, he would ask over and
21 over if he could call. She reported her father did not want him to call his counselor, and he would
22 get tired of hearing ALBERT say "I want to call my counselor" and would hit him. ASHLEY
23 reported, "We are more guilty for the physical abuse than my father is because we would not stop
24 sassing him. CLAIRE and ALBERT in particular would sass my father back, so we are the guilty
25 ones."

"ASHLEY reported to the undersigned that when her father drank alcohol, she would sometimes get afraid because he would act mad. When first asked if there was physical abuse in the home ASHLEY stated, 'My father would not hurt anyone, well maybe the cat.' When asked about if he hurt the cat she responded that he sometimes kicked the cat. She reported that her father gave her brother, ALBERT, seven or eight black eyes, he would slug her brother in the eye. ASHLEY reported she remembers her sister, CLAIRE, having one or two black eyes the father gave CLAIRE when he was mad at her. ASHLEY reported she did not receive any black eyes and she usually did not get in trouble with her father. ASHLEY reported for some reason her father took out most of his anger on ALBERT. She stated ALBERT would 'sass' her father back and her father would get madder and madder at him. ASHLEY reported ALBERT 'kinda deserved' getting hit by her father because he would ask silly things like wanting to call his counselor at school, he would ask over and over if he could call. She reported her father did not want him to call his counselor, and he would get tired of hearing ALBERT say, 'I want to call my counselor' and would hit him. ASHLEY reported, 'We are more guilty for the physical abuse than my father is because we would not stop sassing him. CLAIRE and ALBERT in particular would sass my father back, so we were the guilty ones.'"[13] (Source: California

---

[13] The preceding excerpt includes Ashley mentioning animal abuse. Oftentimes, an abused person may have difficulty discussing harm to themselves or a close loved one, but they may feel more inclined to discuss harm to a pet. Harm to the pet (similar to damaging personal property) can be a

Department of Health and Human Services, Child Protective Services)

I "kinda" created negative situations by talking too much at school. The word "rough" will always have an eerie meaning for me, invoking thoughts of being struck in the head, punched in the stomach, or strangled. I had not yet learned a harsh lesson. I would come to understand that what happens at home stays at home. I also learned to be careful what I say. I am grateful to teach something from it, but as I reflect, I realize that each presentation on abuse I provide is missing a crucial profession in the audience: schoolteachers. So many beatings came pursuant to communication from the school. For me, those damn[14] concerned phone calls were deadly. One of the worst summers I had was when I said, "life was rough," in response to a teacher inquiring how my home life was. It was not the first time I said something at the end of the school year, but each time there was no limit to the severity of punishments I received since I was shielded from prying eyes all summer.

---

message from the abuser saying, "I will do this to you." Conversely, there are situations where an animal is treated better than household members. Either way, the existence of a pet is often an important source for insight into the overall living conditions.

[14] As I write this, I am more upset with myself. I have been making this point for countless years, and I do not recall a teacher attending our domestic violence training. We do not generally picture them as part of a multi-disciplinary team. But are they not mandatory reporters? What percentage of hotline calls come from teachers?

Concerning my statement that life was "rough," the school officials did not know what it meant and decided to call my home to gain clarity and express their concerns. They accomplished something—bravo! My father charismatically alleviated their concerns and my life became all the worse for it. Concerned phone calls can be deadly because they appraise an abuser of what officials find problematic but do nothing to address the underlying conditions creating the concerns in the first place. No treatment, services, or education is provided, and they have advance warning if a hotline call is later made. So, in my humble opinion, it does nothing more than make the caller feel better about themselves, because it certainly is not the best practice for keeping a child safe. I apologize for being glib, but bravo.

Every day I look in the mirror, I am reminded of a beating I got from one of the concerned phone calls. I did not intend to say anything negative about my home environment, but my words were taken the wrong way concerning Ashley. I do not know the extent of what Ashley witnessed or endured. Her experience was different from mine and my older sister's, but that did not make it a better or more tolerable experience. I will not understand our history through her eyes until she is ready to share, if at all. As a child, I wrongly viewed that she was treated differently, but I don't know everything and who knows what would have happened had we not been removed[15] as things had played out?

24   She reported it really scared her when ALBERT would get slugged by Mr. Grieve. CLAIRE
25 stated he would slug ALBERT in the face and in the back. She said ALBERT had probably 10
26 black eyes from Mr. Grieve hitting him in the eye and she stated she had two black eyes from her
27 stepfather. CLAIRE reported it hurt more to get slugged in the back than it did in the eye. CLAIRE
reported she did not know why ASHLEY did not get abused, but she was glad that someone at least

"She reported it really scared her when ALBERT would get slugged by Mr. Grieve. CLAIRE stated he would slug ALBERT in the face and in the back. She said ALBERT had probably 10 black eyes from Mr. Grieve hitting him in the eye and she stated she had two black eyes from her stepfather. CLAIRE reported it hurt more to get slugged in the back than it did in the eye. CLAIR reported she did not know why ASHLEY did not get abused..." (Source: California Department of Health and Human Services, Child Protective Services)

I believe Ashley was in the second grade when she stayed home for an illness. After she had recovered, she asked to remain home, and my father allowed her. When she returned to class, her teacher asked Ashley what was wrong. Ashley advised she was sick, and her teacher inquired further, "Sick with what?" Ashley said, "Sick of

---

[15] As an adult, I expressed my childhood belief that Ashley was favored. I did not mean that as a reflection on her, and I failed to consider how that message would be received, but I still apologized and apologize now. Yet another reason it is easier to run from my past, even if that means not talking to my siblings.

school." I thought my little sister was a handful and casually mentioned to Mr. Hudson, "You're gonna be in trouble next year" (when Ashley moved up to his class).

When I got home from school that day, my father was on the phone. He was sitting on the wooden bench, pulled up to the dining room table. It was an old picnic-style table with long benches, stained dark and varnished (I'll share why this stands out in my memory later). His back was to the wall. The phone was a wall-mounted white corded phone, which he replaced on the hook when he completed the call. I knew the call was about me; I could tell. He ran over to me and threw me on the ground. He sat on my chest and pinned my arms down with his legs. He balled his right hand into a fist and proceeded to pound me in the face. I was unsure what I did wrong at the time, I only knew I could not block, and even the back of my head hurt as I lay there being punched because the carpet was cheap and not well-padded.

I know he did not believe me at first, but I continued to get into trouble even if I did convince him of why I said what I did at school. The lingering pain was probably worse than the initial punishment, and I kept crying. As I cried, I was preventing a large laceration under my eye from healing, and I was supposed to go to school. So, I kept getting disciplined for crying and eating food at home when I could have been receiving free food at school. My sisters would bring home my schoolwork, so I was kept at home until I was mostly healed. When I returned to school, I still had a nasty laceration under my eye and said it was either the cat or my sister.

Flinching was something for which I started getting into trouble as well. Sometimes, the sound of my father's voice would cause me to want to block, and I would reflexively "jump." I do not remember the details, but I guess my father got a call about it because I started getting hit for being "jumpy." I now had to learn how to brace without moving much.

Then there were the regular punishments that left marks. My father had thrown me up against the ceiling before, but then gravity continued his work. I tried hiding under my bed, only to have him hit and poke me with the wooden rod on which people hang clothes.

18 During the course of the investigation, the undersigned has learned that the children have all
19 been exposed to or suffered physical abuse. ALBERT has received, as stated by ALBERT, 10 to 14
20 black eyes. CLAIRE reported she has received at least two black eyes by her father slugging her in
21 the face. All of the children report they are fearful of their father when he drinks because he acts very
22 mean and angry. It was reported to the undersigned that when the father gets drunk, he will wake the
23 children up and make them do chores late at night. It was also reported the father tells CLAIRE that

"During the course of the investigation, the undersigned has learned that the children have all been exposed to or suffered physical abuse. ALBERT has received, as stated by ALBERT, 10 to 14 black eyes. CLAIRE reported she has received at least two black eyes by her father slugging her in the face. All of the children report they are fearful of their father when he drinks because he acts very mean and angry. It was reported to the undersigned that when the father gets drunk, he will wake the children up and make the do

47

chores late at night..." (Source: California Department of Health and Human Services, Child Protective Services)

On occasion, when I hid under the bottom of my bunkbed, if my father was drunk enough, he might not find me. Sometimes, he would think I ran out the front door. He used to become inebriated to the point of urinating on himself. Especially after my mother's homicide, Claire often served as a caretaker, helping him to bathe and such.

Sometimes when my father hit me, I could sort of block and scream like I was really hurt or loud enough that it might disturb the neighbors. I hated getting hit in the face. It hurt and the pain lasted longer. It sucked because I could not hide anywhere, and running away was scary because I didn't know how to provide for myself.

What about looking in the mirror? The scar under my right eye had faded by the time I left high school, but I still have a chipped tooth. Every time I brush my teeth, I think about my father's wrath in response to a teacher's curiosity. It's not triggering or anything—just another memory showing that childhood is painful. I swallowed a good chunk of my lower center right tooth. My wife blames me for our kids needing braces and says my teeth are messed up anyway. It is what it is; a reminder that what happens as home stays at home and be careful what you say. On the positive side, it has helped me as an attorney to be more thoughtful about the words I use and the message I intend to convey. If you look hard enough, there is always a silver lining.

Chapter 5

Creative Punishments

(kree-ey-tiv puhn-ish-muhnts)

What does not kill you makes you stronger...

or it *really* hurts.

Punishments increased in frequency and severity. This necessarily meant that corresponding contacts from the authorities increased as well. Investigations are a two-way street. Whenever the school or Child Protective Services inquired as to what occurred at home, my father took mental notes. I believe his paranoia led him to alter his abusive techniques to avoid detection, but some people are very clever and cunning in concealing abuse, doing so intentionally.

We must get it right the first time because each contact is a learning opportunity for all involved parties. Also of note is that each contact may be initiated by different agencies or personnel within an organization so that a perpetrator may gain more insight than responding individuals. This could mean a new interaction for that responding person, but the abuser may have had multiple distinct contacts[16] by that point. I became more effective with lying during each subsequent contact,[17] and while I did not think the

---

[16] A reminder of why record retention and reviewing history is important.

[17] For what it is worth, I interviewed my father after he was released from prison and asked about his lying to investigators. He claimed he did not prevent anyone from coming and investigating, but he tried to hide what was happening. What stood out to me was that he believed nobody questioned the initial explanation—it was never challenged. Had the explanation been challenged, cracks may have appeared in the story. It is permissible and encouraged to challenge the account of a caregiver (whoever is caring for a child) because we must ensure we are uncovering facts and not merely transcribing lies. Dig for proof that what is being said is accurate.

explanations[18] were that creative, the fabrications worked.

Fv to Mills Middle School, met with minor Albert alone at his election. Minor appeared healthy, was neatly dressed and well groomed. No body check as minor denied abuse and stated that punishments consistent of being denied chocolate. Minor's affect was slightly elevated, it did not change no matter what the subject. Minor appeared to be very charming, and appeared to want to illicit this worker's assistance with obtaining medical services for his father and assisting his father with obtaining telephone access to his sister Claire. As this worker was leaving the school, minor was talking intently with the school secretary.

"Fv to Mills Middle School, met with minor Albert alone *at his election* (emphasis added). Minor appeared healthy, was neatly dressed and well groomed. No body check as minor denied abuse and stated that punishments consistent of being denied chocolate. Minor's affect was slightly elevated, it did not change no matter what the subject. Minor appeared to be very charming and appeared to want to illicit this worker's assistance with obtaining medical services for his father and assisting his father with obtaining telephone access to his sister Claire. As the worker was leaving the school, minor was talking intently with the school secretary." (Source: California Department of Health and Human Services, Child Protective Services)

The most common explanations were that the cat harmed me, or my sister beat me up. Both were often used to explain welts. For the record, belts hurt, extension cords[19] hurt more, but belt buckles

---

[18] We, as children, also learned to start asking to speak to investigators away from everyone, especially my father. Not all children know to do this, but it shows how experienced we were becoming.

[19] According to Claire, my mother beat me with an extension cord once when her grip loosened, and the plug hit me in the

hurt the worst because of welts, bruising, and bleeding. Pain from the metal belt buckle always seemed to linger longer than the sharp pain of the belt or extension cord because the bruises were deeper and throbbed. The same can be said for the beatings I got with the wooden pole in the closet used for hanging clothes. These beatings were the result of my mother trying to be as effective as possible with my punishments, and I do not blame her. Equally impactful were the sounds of the belt or extension cord slicing through the air, almost as chilling as the whack made when striking my bare skin and the resulting shock of pain. None of this was made known at the time to authorities. So, to set the record straight, neither a cat nor my sister scratched the back of my legs above my knees; these were strikes to my rear that hit too low.

I remember selling a story about one of my black eyes: I was running down a hallway, tripped, and my eye socket hit the doorknob. I acted out running down the hallway and clumsily falling into the doorknob. I wanted to impress my father, making him happy by convincing the worker of the lie we created. Frequently, I would devise a story to appease my father (and his concerns that the abuse would be revealed) to prevent further punishments when we believed somebody would be coming after one of those concerned calls home. I always tried to manipulate my father, assuring him I could deal with the situation and make the

---

forehead. Apparently, the bleeding and injury immediately stopped her, and she wanted to take me to get treatment. My father would not let her. My mother was often punished by my father when she took up for me.

worker disappear. When we ultimately had home visits, my father was present—watching and listening. Regardless, the workers always acted as if they cared, but merely took notes and left me there. So, my primary concern was always what would happen after the bubbly investigator left.[20]

The worst punishments always happened during the summer when nobody would know. It was not like we played outside or anything. That dining room table was the source of a lot of pain. My worst beating came as a result of that table. We had come home from shopping, and my father purchased some soda as a rare treat. At the time, we were living at Green Point Apartments. I was standing with my back to the door, at the end of the table, facing the kitchen. I was instructed to stand there and drink the soda. I do not know why and did not mean to do it, but I spilled some soda. I was probably too excited. It ran off the table onto the carpet. Somehow the soda made the finish on the table turn to a whitish color. My father lost it[21]

---

[20] I took great pride in working for Children's Division and what we were trying to do. I have no ill will toward practitioners, but I am trying to convey how I felt as a youth, and I was not as understanding or trusting as I am now.

[21] I purchased two things before the birth of my first son: a reliable vehicle and a steam cleaner. I told myself I would never cry over spilled milk, and I accept that kids will destroy things, hopefully not intentionally. Lives are worth more than material things. We paid too much for that vehicle but kept it for almost eighteen years before selling it. We overpaid for things because my wife and I had "no" credit, not "bad" credit. My wife came from a third-world nation and I came from foster care. Everything we have built has come at a greater expense because we have not had our parents or other relatives' shoulders to stand on—something our children will never have to experience.

and immediately attacked me. He threw me against the ceiling as hard as he could, or at least it felt like that was his intent; I struck it and fell back to the ground.

Then my mother stepped in. Her punishments were worse at times, and this was no exception. She made me get inside a black sleeping bag and zip it all the way up. It was almost like something she had in her playbook that she learned through her own experience. My father attacked me without warning. There was no waiting or anticipation. It was like boom, things are spinning, and you're in shock—go to your happy place. However, with my mother, there was hope that I could convince her to change her mind. There was a discussion as I tried to apologize for spilling the soda, promised to clean it up, and never drink soda again. She remained steadfast and coaxed me into the sleeping bag, all the way, including my head. She then beat me with the wooden pole from the closet.

With each blow to my body, my spirit was crushed, and hope was knocked out of me. Again and again, she struck; it was not apparent how long this would last. It was physically painful, but I had trouble blocking because I did not know from where the hits were coming. Initially, she would hit high, which made me block high, then she would hit lower on my body, and I would try to block there. Eventually, I just shielded my head. What a terrible punishment life was for my transgression of being born. I feel like punishments were designed to inflict as much pain as possible, and this one seemed particularly calculated to strike every vulnerable area. I had lumps all over, but the ones on my face hurt the most. They say soda isn't good for you and that was made very clear. I wish I had never received soda that day.

Even when discipline seemed done, the punishment was never really over. I kept getting disciplined because I could not eat afterward and cried often. You would think it would be okay if I did not eat because missing meals was a distinct punishment. I would apologize for crying, but I had trouble stopping. I think the next day, later in the evening, my father made some rice dish with cheese. Cheese was not something we ate often. It was a big bowl of food which was also unusual. I tried to eat it and I tried not to cry. I feel like the meal was an apology of sorts. It was not like this beating brought me closest to death, strangulation generally held that title, but it is one of the worst beatings I can recall. Once I had almost finished the bowl, I threw it up, all right back in it. At least it was good that my mess was contained. Obviously, I got in trouble again for wasting food— my father thought I was doing it on purpose seeking attention—but I really could not eat. Thankfully, the subsequent punishment was not as bad.

When I got those extremely effective punishments that left visible proof, there was a grace period of sorts. I was spared some of the worst disciplines while I was still healing. I often wanted my punishments to be visible because it put my father on guard for investigators, and there was a potential ceasefire. As I look back, I wanted someone to help and put me in any place better, but when things got real, I always tried to lie. When it really came down to it, I feared the authorities would not remove me, and if they did, it was likely to be worse than the life I knew. Making punishments visible was less effective on long breaks like summer and winter vacations because I was less visible. Besides, punishments began to evolve.

Standing on my head became a punishment. It may seem fun to do as a child, but not if you are forced to do it, especially for long periods. My eyes would get swollen, and my head would hurt (not sure if it was from crying or being on my head for so long). I would fall to the ground for a brief break, get in trouble—hit or something—and then return to standing on my head. An investigator rushing into the house at that moment would have no idea that I had endured strange and unusual punishments,[22] assuming I had merely been crying. This notion would not be refuted absent building trust with the worker where I felt safe to disclose. Sometimes, I would get punched in the stomach or kicked. I hated getting put in the linen closet on a shelf. I would have to ball up and my father would close the door. He forgot I was in there on at least one occasion and apologized. Even if I could reach the doorknob, I dare not escape for fear of being discovered, disciplined more, and then being returned to the closet. Neither of these punishments left visible injuries. If anyone saw me, my face might be red, my eyes

---

[22] A warning sign for extreme abuse, domestic violence, and an increased potential for homicide.

swollen, but nothing in appearance more than crying.

He made me lie in the tub with cold bath water numerous times, with my clothes on. Besides getting into trouble for being sick, I did not care. I tried to make it seem like this was a horrible punishment (so he would use this instead of other stuff), but I do not think it worked. He threw me down on the hallway floor, pulled my pants down, and twisted the shaft of my genitals. That was just weird, but not something I talked about at school. A few times, he put my head in the toilet. If I could have chosen this as a punishment, it probably would have been one of my first choices[23] after the bathtub. Our home was immaculate, and I did not view the toilet, at least in our bathroom, as I do today. It did not seem dirty to me. Other than bumping my head on the bottom of the toilet bowl and the humiliation, I was not hurt. It was not like I was drowning. I used a towel to dry my head off afterward, again crying profusely as if this was the worst punishment imaginable.

The scariest by far was being choked or, as I would learn as a practitioner, strangled. I could not touch my father's hands as he tightly grasped me around the throat and lifted me off the ground. When he tightened his grip, I could not breathe, and I was resigned to looking deep into his cold blue eyes which showed nothing but hate and contempt for my very being. I understood that I could not fight back as he gripped me tighter and

---

[23] I have to express that writing this as a whole just kind of sucks. That's it. Not the most informative footnote.

shook me violently, preventing even a gasp. His spit would land on my face as he cursed at me. I would try to let my hands fall to my sides and take the punishment, forcing my mind to leave the present. How can I escape this life? It was not worth living; the benefits did not outweigh the torment. I do not know how to describe the feeling when you cannot breathe—chest on fire, pleading for air—and you know there is nothing you can do to change that. As my vision started to get fuzzy and dim in those moments, I believe he was deciding whether to put me down like a dog—permanently out of my misery. Was I lucky? Although strangulation would not be my only punishment, he decided not to kill me each time. He would drop me, hit me, and kick me, and I could not block because I would be dizzy and disoriented. My lips would tingle[24] from lack of blood flow. Each time, I am blessed to have survived another punishment. What does not kill you is supposed to make you stronger.

---

[24] I do not have many records to put in this chapter because my father successfully obscured what was happening from prying eyes, aided by the lies of my siblings and me.

Chapter 6

Creative Control

(kree-ey-tiv kuhn-trohl)

"If it's not broken, then" break it.

Growing up, one of my strengths was manipulation. It is a dangerous double-edged sword that can cut the user as quickly as those on the receiving end. When I was eventually removed from my home and entered the system, I would get into trouble for trying to manipulate others. Nobody wants to be used or controlled. Finding out that someone has been manipulative can be very destructive to relationships. Yet, in my home, it was one of the few tools I had available to mitigate the abuse I suffered. Nothing else seemed possible. I was confident the authorities would not help.

I tried to run away from my home once as a child and strongly considered it on another occasion. There were often free lunch programs during the summer, and I was allowed to go to preserve the food we had at home. On one of those summer days, around the fourth grade, my father made me leave the house. It was so unusual because I generally could not go anywhere, and now I could and had no idea where to go. The only place I could think of going was to school. There was a park between the school and the Highway 99 Freeway. I played there for a few hours until I got hungry and bored. Besides, it had those metal slides that burn your skin when it is hot outside. I started wandering further away from my home and found myself in this older gentleman's home, apparently a parent to some children playing in an apartment complex. He gave me something to eat and I thought I could live[25] there—it wasn't too far from my school. After the sun started to set, he told me I had to go home and reality reared its ugly head. I had been gone for hours and nobody was looking for me. I wanted to say I did not feel safe at home, but what was the point? I wandered back home and, once inside, hid in my room. I survived another day.

The time I actually tried to run away, my father and mother had been fighting again. Although, fights always seemed one way—my father relentlessly picked on my mother, especially when in his frequently drunken state. My mother once again mustered the courage to run away. I would appreciate on this day how difficult that was to do. My mother was outside the door, and my father was panicking. I had to retrieve her meds, so my father could show them to the authorities. Each time she ran away, he played the helpless caretaker, dutifully looking after my paranoid mother. It was still a dangerous environment to live in after there was a fear the authorities would come because my father continued to drink. If ever asked, he would say he started drinking because he was upset.

I volunteered to go look for my mother so that I could encourage her to return home and make sure she did not talk. On occasion, I had convinced her to return. I had been with her inside scary and

---

[25] I had a case as a Guardian ad Litem, where I put the child I represented in touch with a close friend as a mentor. When the mentor called, the child asked if they were going to be living with a mentor. I know that feeling of longing for a home, almost any home.

uncomfortable battered spouse's shelters. On this day, however, I had no intention of looking for her. I just wanted to leave, and the safest[26] way was with his permission. I had to be eleven or twelve during this episode. I remember once being allowed to leave feeling a sense of freedom, with no destination in mind.

I left our apartment off Martin Luther King Jr. Blvd., near 47th Avenue, in Sacramento. It used to be called Green Point and was referred to by some as "gunpoint." It seemed that a Sacramento County Sheriff helicopter would fly over the complex every day, shining down a spotlight for at least a half hour—yet nobody saw me. Outside of a few bullies who harassed me to and from school, I did not feel uncomfortable[27] there. Surely it could not be any worse than what transpired inside my home.

I walked along side streets until I reached Franklin Blvd., and then headed north. There was a giant Campbell's Soup factory on Franklin. As I understood it, they would cook one soup on a given day. Generally, I enjoyed the smells emanating

---

[26] I thrived in chaos because I felt it was the only time my father valued me. For some reason, during these types of events, he listened to me. That led to me causing chaos once I was a ward of the state so I could try to direct and control my environment. This type of manipulation was frowned upon.

[27] To this day, I feel more out of place, and therefore uncomfortable, in more affluent areas. For instance, my car was stolen (twice) in the St. Louis area when I was an insurance claims adjuster. Against counsel, I traveled with a friend to recover some of the stolen contents from a high-crime inner city St. Louis location. We came up empty handed for the record.

from the facility. On this day, the smells served only to remind me that I would have nothing to eat if I left home.

As I continued walking, I believed someone would see me, stop to check on me, and make everything okay. With each passing vehicle, my hope waned—I was invisible. I dreamed a lot. Life in my fictitious world was always so preferable to real life. Every day that passed reinforced my understanding that nobody was coming to save the day. It became clear on this day that nobody who passed me knew me or what I was going through. Nobody was going to give me a handout. Nobody cared or knew enough to care. I passed by St. Patrick's Thrift Store and St. Rose's Catholic Church. Still, not a single person came to my aid; everybody was busily going about their perfect lives.

The thrift store reminded me I no longer had one of my favorite toys. I didn't have many toys, but I did have a white metal tow truck with blue plastic trim purchased from the thrift store. I fashioned a tow hook with a string and a paper clip. I also had some cheap plastic army figurines that were all one color. Our carpet had been replaced a couple of years prior and my father packed toys into a black trash bag. I figured it was to get them out of the way while the carpet was replaced. I helped put toys in the bag, which seemed to please him. Then, he told me to take the bags to the dumpster. I cried, but I was instructed to leave everything in the bag. I learned attachment to items like toys was a bad thing.

As I wandered the street, I had nothing beyond the clothes on my back. It was a chilly and overcast day. The ground was wet. I wore a light jacket, high-water blue jeans, and some black tennis shoes from Payless Shoe Source. I began thinking about how I would provide for myself. Maple Elementary School was a little east of Franklin Blvd. I went to a drinking fountain at the school to quench my thirst. I had water covered but still needed food and somewhere to sleep. It had outdoor corridors with roofs but no walls. At least it could shield me from the rain.

I started walking north again and passed Roma's Pizzeria. The food there always smelled good. I remember getting food from there once or twice. I remember their minestrone. It seemed like a lot of broth with very little food inside, but it tasted good. I still have fond memories of it. But on this day, it was simply another smell that made me hungry.

I turned east through a residential neighborhood and found a shopping cart from Harvest Foods. I discovered a way to provide for myself! These carts must cost a lot of money, and surely, I could receive compensation. I should at least be able to get a soda. However, as I approached the store, I soon realized that nobody would know I recovered this cart for the store, finding it in some residential neighborhood. As I approached the parking lot, I observed patrons returning carts to the store. I entered the store with the shopping cart, and nobody paid me any mind. Nobody ever did. Nobody knew I existed.

I started walking back home along Franklin but happened upon the police station. Maybe, just maybe, it was time to come clean to the authorities. I was tired of carrying all these dirty secrets. I wanted to report everything I had witnessed and endured—spill everything! I entered the police station and observed someone who appeared to be a sergeant behind a desk speaking on the phone. He took a pause from the conversation, pulled the phone away from his ear, and asked me if I was Albert looking for my mother. I said I was, learning that this sergeant was on the phone with my father! The sergeant informed me that my father was worried about me. It was a sign I could not miss, so I told him I was returning home. My father was everywhere. There was no escape.

Whenever my mother would run away, which seemed to be every six months or so, my father would report her missing. Since she took medications, he would tell the authorities that she was crazy, parading around her medications. It also did not help that she would often be institutionalized until she recanted.

Interview of Mrs. Grieve was actually conducted by phone since she was hospitalized at the time ▮▮▮▮▮▮▮▮▮▮ Mother denied any domestic violence or alcohol abuse by the father. She completely recanted her statement and said that it was made when she wasn't on her medication so she didn't know what she was saying. Mother was very concerned that her kids were going to be removed.

"Interview of Mrs. Grieve was actually conducted by phone since she was hospitalized at the time...Mother denied any domestic violence or alcohol abuse by the father. She completely recanted her statement and said that it was made when she wasn't on her medication so she didn't know what she was saying. Mother was very concerned that her kids were going to be removed." (Source: California Department of Health and Human Services, Child Protective Services)

My father, being a white[28] male veteran looking out for a crazy black woman, would almost always win over the authorities. There was one time that he was arrested for domestic violence, but this was the exception to the rule, and we bonded him out the same night. I believe he was arrested because there was so much property damage, including the Christmas tree being knocked over, that the police could not just walk away.

My only option for safety was creatively controlling whatever I could, often through manipulation. In the fifth grade, I was suspended for getting into a fight. At first, I avoided getting into trouble at home, but it was only a reprieve. I got into an argument with this kid named Emmanual. I bested him in a battle of words, so he threatened to beat me up at recess. Recess came, and he sure enough tried. He was larger than me —tall and skinny. He cornered me in a field behind the bungalows and pushed me to the ground. As I lay on my back, I kept kicking my feet at him so he could not get on top of me to pummel me (I

---

[28] My elementary school once called or threatened to call the police on my father because he threatened and berated the school for labeling me as black on a standardized test. There were many situations and statements which demonstrated his prejudice, but I never understood why he stayed.

recalled my father doing it, which was very unpleasant). Unable to get past my guard, he backed off. I took the opportunity to flee back toward the classrooms.

I was often in the computer room after completing my schoolwork before others. I knew a baseball bat was in the computer room and asked the computer teacher to borrow it. It caused him to pause as it was an unusual request, especially from someone like me who does not play sports. Yet he trusted me and allowed me to take the bat. I found Emmanual on the playground and started running after him, screaming and swinging the baseball bat. Eventually, the computer teacher learned of my antics and took the bat. In class, threats were renewed, and I wanted to get ahead of them. In front of the teacher and everyone, I picked up a chair and cracked Emmanual over the head, hitting him with the metal leg. We were both sent to the office and suspended. He never bothered me again, but now I had to face my father.

I slowly walked home. I had to convince my father not to beat me. As I reached the door, I had an idea. He opened the door, and I yelled, "That motherf***ker was talking about you, so I beat him up." It was risky, but the fact that he had never heard me curse probably sold the lie. At first, he did not know what to do. Then, he was overcome with something I had rarely seen: pride. I did not get into trouble because he thought I was defending his honor. As time passed, however, and I did not go to school the next day, things returned to normal. Now, he had to see me all day or at least know I was home. I wanted to eat food instead of having free lunch, and any momentary pride he had concerning my violent acts of aggression at school yielded to his hatred for my being.

Some creative control techniques are less pleasant to share. Initially, I don't know if it was intentional or involuntary. There was this constant battle between my parents trying to beat me in undetectable ways and my attempts to inflict self-harm. I learned with evident and severe injuries, there was a grace period before subsequent beatings. For instance, I would lie on the dining room table's bench with my head under the table while beaten with a belt or an extension cord. When struck, I would jump, and the back of my head would hit the underside of the table. This could result in an injury that someone could see, and my spanking would stop. Once I realized this, I would bang my head with every spanking. Since we were in the apartment, I was also screaming too loud, posing another problem for my parents (not that anyone ever did anything about the noise). Sometimes, I would be made to put a sock in my mouth before the beating began so others could not hear me. It seemed the planned punishments were the worst.

My overweight mother came up with a creative solution to counter my actions. She would lay me down on the king-sized mattress in their bedroom and sit on the back of my head and torso, smashing me into the bed. My screams were significantly muffled since it was hard enough to breathe. Nothing could stop this beating. All the marks left would be underneath my clothes which nobody checked. All I could do was go to some safe place in my mind, ignoring what was physically occurring until something happened that made the beating stop. While lying on the bed, she smothered me into the mattress, beating my bare rear. My pants and underwear were around my ankles, and suddenly I defecated—the beating stopped. At that moment, I had discovered a new way to lessen the punishments.

Chapter 7

The Hammer

(thuh ham-er)

"Caution! Slow down! Kids" are not at play...

Julie and Cecil Palmer, Managers, Mills Tower Apartments, 362-2814:

Mrs. Palmer described this family as "very, very odd." When asked what she meant by very odd, she reported the whole family appeared to be "paranoid." When the father would come out of the apartment building, he would look, over his shoulder as if someone was coming after him. When the children went to school every morning, they went through the back of the apartment and it appeared they did not want to have contact with anyone on the courtyard of the complex. Mr. and

"<u>Julie and Cecil Palmer, Managers, Mills Tower Apartments, 362-2814</u>: Mrs. Palmer described this family as 'very, very odd.' When asked what she meant by very odd, she reported the whole family appeared to be 'paranoid.' When the father would come out of the apartment building, he would look, over his shoulder as if someone was coming after him. When the children went to school every morning, they went through the back of the apartment and it appeared they did not want to have contact with anyone on the courtyard of the complex..." (Source: California Department of Health and Human Services, Child Protective Services)

To say that we were isolated would be a tremendous understatement. With nobody to see what was happening behind closed doors, and even if somebody did see, with nobody who would save us, we were forced to do things we otherwise would not. I have so many memories I am not fond of, heavy suffocating guilt from my actions of self-preservation. Self-harm or defecating is one thing but manipulating chaotic situations to redirect attention away from me is shameful as I look back. Unfortunately, it gets worse than that.

During one drunken episode, my father made me do something I will never forget. He was making burritos for dinner, or more accurately, commanding that Claire make the dinner, and she was failing to meet his OCD standards. He grabbed a hammer and told me to hit my sister with it. I had no idea where my mother was, if she was even in the house. Although the decision was made in the blink of an eye, the vivid memory haunts me for all eternity.

I could have chosen to refuse, to take the punishment. Someone on the outside may say from their infinite wisdom and lack of relatable experiences that I should have hit my father. Perhaps I would be incarcerated, but my mother would still be alive. Unfortunately, we were programmed. We had this blind obedience where we generally did what we were told.

In Chapter 3, I mentioned an incident with a screwdriver. After my father was arrested for domestic violence before Christmas one day, he took the only car keys with him to jail. Our neighbor started the car we had with a screwdriver and took my mother to bond out my father. To my knowledge, my mother did not have a driver's license.

Fast forward a week or two, and we were loading up the car to go to the California Exposition Center (CalExpo) for free toys. I entered the rear driver-side seat and instinctually reached for the door handle as my father's arm remained extended between the door and the roof rail. I think he was reaching for a seat belt, but I stopped before attempting to close the door since his arm was in the way. Then he told me, "Close the door." I complied by pulling the door handle even though his arm was still there. The door crushed his arm, or at least hurt quite a bit. I failed as a child to understand the concept of sarcasm. Now, I am confused and in trouble for doing as instructed, stemming from my fear of getting punished for disobedience. I blindly did what he told me without considering if it was right or wrong, as expected, but he was mad because I should have ignored him.

He did not seek medical treatment but complained the entire way to CalExpo. My mother took my sisters to the event center to wait in a long line for free toys. Instead, I was stuck in the back of the car, seat belt on, as my father continuously berated me—stabbing me in the stomach with the screwdriver used to operate the vehicle. He pushed the screwdriver harder as I tried to suck in my gut, stopping short of making me bleed, but my fear did not lessen. It was just another Christmas.

So, on the night we were making burritos, I had instilled within me this programming of blind obedience. It was like I was in a vehicle, but I was not the one steering. I felt I had no choice, no say. My father handed me a hammer and told me to hit my older sister. I was scared. I would have preferred not to eat anything for dinner. I did not need burritos. I wanted everything to stop, but it never[29] does. I had learned the tough way the purpose of punishments was to inflict the maximum possible pain while still allowing

---

[29] Present tense.

consciousness. Add to this that I always got disciplined because nothing I did was ever good enough. I would always be punished for failing to meet my father's extremely high, and as I look back, unattainable standards.

Hammer in hand, I had to inflict pain to perfection or suffer consequences. I turned it to the claw side and began striking my older sister on her back. She screamed out in pain. I was not mad or upset with my sister, and I had no desire to cause her harm, but I put my well-being over hers and did as my father had instructed. What type of person forces a human to commit an act like this against another? What kind of person complies? How do you live with this? I repeatedly struck my sister with the hammer, trying to complete the task perfectly. I feel like this was an act of cowardice. I alone was holding the hammer. I will forever relive this experience, knowing I had a choice, even though I was a child. I can tell myself had I not complied, I would likely have been punished and made to do it anyway, but this still brings no comfort. I now had another layer of guilt that would prevent disclosure. I do not remember if we ate dinner that night, but no meal is worth this price. I did not deserve to eat. I was no better than my father by carrying out his deeds. I do remember portions of her shirt stuck to the blood on her back as she took off the shirt.

This was not the only violent episode concerning a hammer. When I was thirteen, our family had the second to last explosive domestic violence episode I remember. It would be the last opportunity to intervene before the homicide. I talk about this episode during presentations and often forget to point out creative treatment I received earlier in the day. By far, I received the most physical punishments, but my father had become very imaginative by this point in ensuring the harm was only minimally visible. I cannot tell what my offense was that day, but he turned on the electric oven and shoved my head and shoulders inside. I think it was only set to 200 degrees, but it was still hot, and I still was terribly frightened. I tried to avoid touching any of the metal surfaces. As I recall, he pulled out the racks before turning it on. I never got burned, so there were no marks for CPS to discover[30] if they cared to look.

He then put Tapatio hot sauce in my eyes. That was very uncomfortable, and I was crying uncontrollably. He had a change of heart and said he would rinse out my eyes. He used Windex. I think my mother later tried to help me wash my eyes out with water while I pretended to have trouble seeing. I was fine with a little self-harm to sell it. How would CPS not come if I showed up to school blind? Maybe that would be enough? If things got a little worse, then would somebody

---

[30] Very recently, I was speaking with a manager over social workers recounting an experience with a new hire. On one of their first solo calls, an investigator went to a home for suspicious marks on a child. They returned with positive news, claiming everything was okay (after a wonderful conversation with the caregiver). When asked if the child had marks, the investigator indicated they did not know because they did not check (due to the conversation). In this case, the follow-up in the office ensured this mistake did no go unresolved, but what about in places with less oversight? Was the charismatic caregiver's conversation an acquired skill honed over the course of multiple contacts?

help? The subsequent violent episode between my parents may have resulted from the day's events concerning my punishments. She often got into trouble for trying to protect me, with his hatred then redirected at her.

On this day, my mother escaped the apartment. Once in the courtyard, she just started screaming. She did not bother running anywhere; it never worked out for her anyway. My father grabbed a hammer and tried to get her to stop screaming and make her come inside. She would not. Then he cracked her in the forehead with the hammer I had used on my sister. I do not remember if this made her stop screaming or not; I was still pretending to be blind, that is, until the ambulance came. Someone in the apartment building finally called the authorities, but I only remember an ambulance—I do not recall the police (and do not see evidence of an arrest in any of the documents I obtained).

Our apartment building was shaped like a rectangular donut, with every apartment facing the pool in the center of the courtyard. We never used the pool. I'm sure our neighbors noticed that. They certainly had a front-row seat to this evening's most recent domestic violence episode, and I'm glad someone finally did something about it by simply calling[31] 911.

---

[31] There is a domestic violence PSA video I received from another trainer, made by the United Nations. In the video, a couple is eating a meal in quiet except for the sounds of a couple arguing violently next door. They exchange uncomfortable glances but continue eating in silence. At one point, the arguing couple crashes into the wall next to the couple eating their food. The man gets up abruptly and grabs

I informed my father that my vision had returned, volunteering to travel in the ambulance with my mother, ensuring she would not talk to anybody. I was allowed to go. It seemed my father hated my existence, but he trusted me as his little helper during these chaotic episodes. The only way he would value me was if there was some horribly violent and traumatic event where I could utilize my manipulative ways. It's so ironic that my mother was diagnosed with paranoid schizophrenia, but the person most paranoid was always my father. When he was the most vulnerable and had no control—my mother running away or screaming for her life, with the authorities coming imminently—who else could he turn to? He could only rely on his little helper, who he knew would comply with any of his orders because he beat that programming into me. At times, I longed for chaos because there was a chance I would be safe if I could keep my father focused on anyone but me. Essentially, I had to choose between decisions that created pain or guilt.

It was challenging to write this chapter, so I almost forgot to talk about what the authorities did. I mentioned this was the last opportunity to intervene because it became another incident rationalized and dismissed by those who could have helped. As a practitioner, I know it is so hard to help when you feel both hands are tied behind

---

a baseball bat before heading next door. He knocks on the door and hands the other guy the bat saying, "Thought you could use this." The message is "do nothing and you might as well lend a hand." In my case, it was a hammer. (Source: UNIFEM, "Lend a Hand"; 10-17-2005)

your back while lacking resources or support to do the job your heart compels you to do. However, as a child, I didn't know the social workers charged to help me were struggling.

The following are excerpts from the CPS investigation. When I first started reading this, hope began to emerge.

Interview with Albert - Child is extremely parentified and controlling. Says his father told the children he was going to swing at her to get her to come into the house but worker didn't believe this to be true. It seemed as if the child was lying to protect his father. Said after the hammer incident, his mother took him with her to the shelter.

"Interview with Albert – Child is extremely parentified and controlling. Says his father told the children he was going to swing at her to get her to come into the house but worker didn't believe this to be true. It seemed as if the child was lying to protect his father. Said after the hammer incident, his mother took him with her to the shelter." (Source: California Department of Health and Human Services, Child Protective Services)

I felt I was better at lying and manipulating than my sisters, and I was encouraged to see the worker saw through the deception.

Interview w/Claire - Says her mother ran into the hammer. Says fa. did not tell the kids what he was going to do with the hammer before he did it. Says her father drinks alcohol about once a month.

"Interview w/Claire – Says her mother ran into the hammer. Says fa. did not tell the kids what he was going to do with the hammer before he did it. Says her father drinks alcohol about once a month." (Source:

California Department of Health and Human
Services, Child Protective Services)

Interview w/Ashley - Says her father was frustrated and just trying to get their mother to come into the house. Says he didn't swing it, but rather her mother jumped up into the hammer causing her injury.

"Interview w/Ashley – Says her father was frustrated and just trying to get their mother to come into the house. Says he didn't swing it, but rather her mother jumped up into the hammer causing her injury." (Source: California Department of Health and Human Services, Child Protective Services)

And then all hope was shattered, the remains cremated, and those ashes cast into the ocean.

Family refuses any services and children do not seem emotionally harmed by the incident whatsoever. Case to be closed.

"Family refuses any services and children do not seem emotionally harmed by the incident whatsoever. Case to be closed." (Source: California Department of Health and Human Services, Child Protective Services)

With this incident, the District Attorney (DA) was in contact with CPS; similar findings suggest that at least. You may find yourself reading the end of this twice.

"Emotional Abuse secondary to domestic violence: Mom is paranoid schizophrenic and on...She was receiving Psych services through...and was doing better, however, her abusive husband had problems with her receiving counseling Tx and actively undermined mom's efforts i.e. he would dictate to her how many sessions she could attend etc. and he himself was not amenable to services. So mom is no longer coming in for her therapy with the reporter. Hx of domestic violence in July '98 dad hit mom on the head with hammer. Mom ended up separating from him and dad had the kids with him. Apparently kids witnessed that violent episode. Dad is legal custodian of the kids due to mom's mental health condition. Mom returned to dad on 8/10/98 and DA dropped charges against him as mom did not wish to pursue due to fear that if dad ended up in jail (which was a possibility), there would be no one to care for the kids (as she does not have custody) and kids would have been placed in foster care...there may be future domestic violence episode which may place mom and kids at risk. Reporter stated at present she does not have any info re: abuse of kids. Her concerns are mom back with dad and no therapy. Note* dad also drinks and in the past violence escalated due to dad's drunkenness." (Source: California Department of Health and Human Services, Child Protective Services)

My mother was again placed in a mental institution for this episode. It had gotten to the point where a nurse was coming to our home weekly to administer Haldol shots because my mother was deemed so delusional with her claims that her husband was trying to kill her and harm her children (that is until she was forced to recant each time she was placed in a mental institution). However, after that last incident, medical staff were afraid to come into our home. At least someone was able to stay safe.

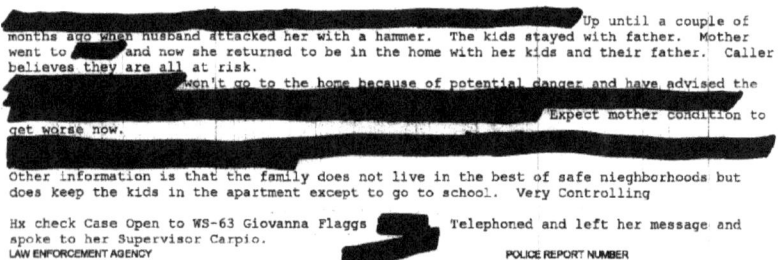

"…Up until a couple of months ago when husband attacked her with a hammer. The kids stayed with father. Mother went to…and now she returned to be in the home with her kids and their father. Caller believes they are all at risk…won't go to the home because of potential danger and have advised the…Expect mother condition to get worse now...Other information is that the family does not live in the best of safe neighborhoods but does keep the kids in the apartment except to go to school. Very Controlling..." (Source: California Department of Health and Human Services, Child Protective Services)

This is as good a point as any to point out how well my father weaponized my mother's mental health while he largely concealed his issues. Each time, when her claims of domestic violence were not believed, her only ticket home was to say she was off her meds, made it all up, and ultimately, each time she recanted. To be clear, my mother was seen as delusional for claiming her husband is trying to kill her, then hospitalized and drugged for these delusions. The only way to get out of being hospitalized was to recant, which reinforced the perception of delusions. But a simultaneous narrative of escalating violence in the home was ever-present. The excerpt below spells out how practitioners were afraid to drug my mother for her delusions of feeling unsafe because they (the practitioners) felt unsafe after my father attacked my mother with a hammer. The icing on the cake is that CPS did not view this environment as being detrimental to us children, just documented that adults who care for people with mental disorders felt it was detrimental to go into this environment.

September 3, 1998: A mandated reporter reported the mother was receiving Haldol injections but after the father attacked the mother with a hammer, the providers would not go to the home because of potential danger. The reporter expects the mother's condition to get worse without the Haldol shots. Children's Protective Services investigator was unable to substantiate a detriment to the children.

"September 3, 1998: A mandated reporter reported the mother was receiving Haldol injections but after the father attacked the mother with a hammer, the providers would not go to the home because of potential danger. The reporter expects the mother's condition to get worse without the Haldol shots. Children's Protective Services investigator was unable to substantiate a detriment to the children." (Source: California Department of Health and Human Services, Child Protective Services)

The following record, created after her death, still cites medication non-compliance as the primary issue. The sad truth is that she constantly feared for her and her children's lives.

8   The undersigned went to Sacramento Mental Health Department and reviewed records regarding

9   Douglas Grieve. Mr. Grieve had been taken to the Sacramento Mental Health Center on April 16,

10 1997. He was given a diagnosis of axis one: alcohol dependency and alcohol intoxication, axis two:

    personality disorder not otherwise specified, axis three: none. He was discharged on April 17, 1999,

11 with a referral to Oak Park Counseling to address alcohol dependency. It was reported the father had

12 armed himself with a knife and said that he was going to kill himself and told his wife and his

13 children that he was going to kill himself. 911 was called and he had been taken for a "5150"

14 evaluation although as mentioned earlier, let go the following day.

15   The undersigned also reviewed the reports from Sacramento Mental Health regarding Bridgett

16 Grieve. She had been admitted to Sacramento Mental Health for 13 occasions between May, 1993

17 and September, 1998. Most of her visits to Sacramento Mental Health were due to her not taking her

18 medication (medication non-compliance) and her becoming psychotic. In 1983, the mother was

19 diagnosed as Manic Depressive and later that diagnosis was changed to Schizophrenia.

20   Weave, Brenda Harris, 920-1781:

21   Ms. Harris reported to the undersigned that Bridgett Grieve had been referred to the WEAVE

22 Safehouse on three occasions. Ms. Harris reported she had no doubt the mother was experiencing

23 domestic violence and was afraid of her husband, Mr. Grieve, and feared for the safety of the

24 children due to physical abuse. The mother was first at the WEAVE Safehouse January 25, 1996 to

25 January 28, 1996. The second admittance was November 4, 1997 to November 8, 1997, and her last

    admission was July 7, 1998 to July 10, 1998.

26

"The undersigned went to Sacramento Mental Health Department and reviewed records regarding Douglas Grieve. Mr. Grieve had been taken to the Sacramento Mental Health Center on April 16, 1997. He was given a diagnosis of axis one: alcohol dependency and alcohol intoxication, axis two: personality disorder not otherwise specified, axis three: none. He was discharged on April 17, 1999, with a referral to Oak Park Counseling to address alcohol dependency. It was reported the father had armed himself with a knife and said that he was going to kill himself. 911 was called and he had been taken for a '5150' evaluation although as mentioned earlier, let go the following day.

The undersigned also reviewed the reports from Sacramento Mental Health regarding Bridgett Grieve. She had been admitted to Sacramento Mental Health for 13 occasions between May, 1993 and September, 1998. Most of her visits to Sacramento Mental Health were due to her not taking her medication (medication non-compliance) and her becoming psychotic. In 1983, the mother was diagnosed as Manic Depressive and later that diagnosis was changed to Schizophrenia.

Weave, Brenda Harris, 920-1781: Ms. Harris reported to the undersigned that Bridgett Grieve has been referred to WEAVE Safehouse on three occasions. Ms. Harris reported she had no doubt the mother was experiencing domestic violence and was afraid of her husband, Mr. Grieve, and feared for the safety of the children due to physical abuse. The mother was first at the WEAVE Safehouse January 25, 1996 to January 28, 1996. The second admittance was November 4, 1997 to November 8, 1997, and her last admission was July 7, 1998 to July 10, 1998." (Source: California Department of Health and Human Services, Child Protective Services)

That last sentence reiterates how she was again placed in a mental institution for the hammer

86

episode, yet nothing was done to address why she fled her apartment and was screaming for help. The truth is, there would be no help[32] for my mother. How many others must share this fate? Until people like me speak up and society at large makes these issues a priority besides an annual frame on a social media profile picture, we will continue to turn a blind eye to the events described in the following chapters.

---

[32] I can do nothing else but pray this book illuminates these issues so that others may receive the help that proved so elusive during my childhood.

Chapter 8

Wings (1961-1998)

(wingz)

"If you love someone, let them go…"

That's it. You don't kill them.

To the very end and beyond, the system[33] got it wrong. It is incredibly frustrating to see what made it into my official record regarding the circumstances leading to and around my mother's death. My mother could care less about marks on the walls or damage to the paint. We truly believed, to our core, that my father would one day kill us and that there were no authorities who cared enough to intervene. So many altercations happened where we were trying to flee to safety within the confines of our apartment. These acts lead to personal property damage and damage to the structure (the walls, doors, etcetera). My father knew that when the authorities routinely came to see what was going on, damage to personal property, doors, and claw marks on the walls all would be things that could lead to questions. Questions were dangerous because they could lead to discovery. So, my father did everything he could to prevent questions and dispel any concerns authorities might have. So no, my mother was not upset about some conflict with the landlord about paint.

---

[33] I apologize in advance for the way I present information in this chapter. I was processing much of the information contained herein along with newly discovered record excerpts. I had to step away several times, returning to "soften" my views on why things transpired as they did.

13 | 1. **PRIOR HISTORY:**

14   On April 7, 1999, the children,███████GRIEVE, age 11 years; ALBERT GRIEVE, age 14

15 | years; and ███████YOUNG, age 17 years, were placed into Protective Custody by Emergency

16 | Response Social Worker, ███Thurston, for allegations of neglect and emotional abuse. According

17 | to the Protective Custody Report, the child, █████████, is suffering severe emotional mental

18 | trauma due to the recent homicide of her mother, Bridgett Grieve. The stepfather, Douglas Grieve, is

19 | denying medical/mental health services for the child. Additionally, all three children had witnessed

20 | the homicide of their mother in which their father was involved. Secondly, the children were at risk

21 | of physical harm due to the history of the father perpetrating domestic violence and child abuse.

22 | Furthermore, the father has a history of alcohol abuse from which he had failed to rehabilitate.

23   According to the Dependent Intake report written by Sheilah Paschall, it was reported the children

24 | had suffered serious emotional trauma directly resulting from their participating in the death of their

25 | mother on December 5, 1998, ruled by the Sacramento County Coroner's Office as homicide. The

26 | mother, Bridgett Grieve, had a documented history of mental health problems and institutionalization.

27 | The mother started to act out because she was upset about a conflict with the landlord about paint.

"PRIOR HISTORY: On April 7, 1999, the children...GRIEVE, age 11 years, ALBERT GRIEVE, age 14 years; and...YOUNG, age 17 years, were placed into Protective Custody by Emergency Response Social Worker,... Thurston, for allegations of neglect and emotional abuse. According to the Protective Custody Report, the child...is suffering severe emotional mental trauma due to the recent homicide of her mother, Bridgett Grieve. The stepfather, Douglas Grieve, is denying medical/mental health services for the child. Additionally, all three children had witnessed the homicide of their mother in which their father was involved. Secondly, the children were at risk of physical harm due to the history of the father perpetrating domestic violence and child abuse. Furthermore, the father has a history of alcohol abuse from which he had failed to rehabilitate.

91

According to the Department Intake report written by Sheilah Paschall, it was reported the children had suffered serious emotional trauma directly resulting from their participating in the death of their mother on December 5, 1998, ruled by the Sacramento County Coroner's Office as homicide. The mother, Bridgett Grieve, had a documented history of mental health problems and institutionalization. The mother started to act out because she was upset about a conflict with the landlord about paint." (Source: California Department of Health and Human Services, Child Protective Services)

The mother started to climb out of a bedroom window, and the family did not want her institutionalized over the holidays. Therefore, the father, Doug Grieve, and the children held her down and physically sat on her. Then with belts and ties, they tied her hands and ankles behind her back and continued to physically sit on her. Due to her loud protest, a decision was made to place a gag in her mouth. A pair of socks was placed in her mouth and was secured by a shirt, which covered the "gag" and was tied around her head. The family left the room and when their father returned to check on her, he discovered that she was dead. According to the family, the mother expired not long after the gag was in place. The father, who had already been drinking, reportedly proceeded to drink three additional bottles of wine. The children constructed a shrine with lit candles placed around their mother's body and slept with the corpse throughout the night into the early afternoon before the father walked them to the local Fire Department to notify authorities of their mother's death.

"The mother started to climb out of a bedroom window, and the family did not want her institutionalized over the holidays. Therefore, the father, Doug Grieve, and the children held her down and physically sat on her. Then with belts and ties, they tied her hands and ankles behind her back and continued to physically sit on her. Due to her loud protest, a decision was made to place a gag in her mouth. A pair of socks was placed in her mouth and was secured by a shirt, which covered the 'gag' and was tied around her head. The family left the room and when their father returned to check on her, he discovered that she was dead. According to the family, the mother expired not long after the gag was in place. The father, who had already been drinking, reportedly proceeded to drink three additional bottles of wine. The children constructed a shrine with lit candles placed around their mother's body and slept with the corpse throughout the night into the early afternoon before the father walked them to the local Fire Department to notify authorities of their mother's death." (Source: California Department of Health and Human Services, Child Protective Services)

I seriously doubt my father drank three bottles of wine after my mother's death. Could he have consumed a lot of box wine before and leading up to the end of my mother? Absolutely. So, this was a typical day with my father being highly intoxicated and getting violent with my mother. Perhaps it was because he was trying to cover up damage from a previous altercation, and my mother could not obtain paint from the landlord because we went to them so frequently (which in and of itself should have been seen as highly unusual).

My mother was trying to escape on this night because she again feared for her life. After trying to escape out the front door, she tried to flee through a bedroom window. My father did not want her to escape because it would lead to the authorities coming (it had nothing to do with the holidays); therefore, he tried to restrain her. Someone who is hysterically trying to save their own life is difficult to control, so my father commanded my siblings and me to help hold her and to obtain belts and stuff to tie her up. Yet again, I was too cowardly to run or to aid my mother—blind obedience. Instead, I feared for my well-being and complied with my father's demands. I do not know who grabbed what or in what ways my siblings and I assisted him, but we complied.

Gags were not abnormal in our household. I endured some of my worst beatings with a sock in my mouth so that people could not hear me scream. I could still breathe through my nose. I do not think the gag caused my mother's death or her weight while lying on her stomach after having her arms and legs tied behind her back (as suggested in the records I obtained). These types of things had happened before. My mother tried to escape countless times. My father had successfully prevented her from trying to escape on numerous occasions. Occasionally, it was because she could not reach an escape quick enough, and he beat her into submission, but he had held her down and restrained her often. I have a vivid memory of my mother laying naked on the floor, just outside the bathroom door, screaming as my father attacked her. This was not an unusual scene.

This day brought a higher level of anger from my father toward my mother. It was more like a deep hatred where he despised her existence. She was trapped between the king-size bed and the wall, lying in the narrow walkway underneath the window with her head pointing toward the corner of the room near the foot of the bed. When my mother was tied up and could go nowhere, lying on her stomach, my father stood on the back of her head. He placed his hands on the adjoining wall as he faced the corner. He pressed his weight onto the back of her head and then jumped up and down. He then spat on her. Is this how someone would protect her from being institutionalized over the holidays?

My mother soiled herself. Later, my father discovered she was dead. He cried, but I do not know why (I assume he feared the consequences). We were made to construct a shrine to memorialize her. After making arrangements for our cat, we went to the fire department. Documentation shows he thought he would be arrested, but he appeared immune from arrest.[34] The firefighters carried my mother out in the same hog-tied position in which she had perished. This is how I learned what rigor mortis was.

Not until later that evening did the Sacramento County Sheriff bring us downtown to be

---

[34] It blows my mind that after my older sister disclosed the sexual abuse, and he corroborated the accounts, they let him go. Read the excerpt at the end of this chapter. It was about a week later when he was finally taken into custody.

interrogated. I was hungry and thirsty, but we were basically left to fend for ourselves. I remember some of those coin candy dispensers, and I was checking inside for candy that had been left behind from someone else's purchase. Someone gave us a little bit of money, and we (my younger sister and I) bought some pop tarts from a vending machine. Then we were separated and individually interrogated. I was asked what happened and had to go through the story repeatedly, each time I told the story as instructed by my father. I had no advocate or Guardian[35] ad Litem. It was just me sitting across the table from two detectives.

Eventually, we took a break, and my father entered the room. He told me to tell the truth so we could go home because my story was the only one that wasn't lining up. I sat in that bare intimidating room with a camera looking at me, trying to read my father's facial expressions and figure out what I was supposed to say. I did not like being in the room or being interrogated. I was hungry, thirsty, and tired, but I was not afraid of those detectives. I feared I would suffer the same fate as my mother, so I had to do what my father wanted me to do. It was just that I didn't know what that was. I had dutifully maintained the story he wanted me to give, and now he's telling me to do something different. I started subtly changing the facts to something more akin to the truth;

---

[35] I am a Guardian ad Litem. I keep a very small caseload so I can really get to know the children for whom I advocate.

apparently, it was enough[36] for the detectives. As I feared, we went home. My father could do anything he wanted to us, and nothing in this world could stop him. You would think there would be justice for my mother. My father believed he would be arrested after he killed her, but nothing changed after her life was stolen.

Collateral: ...ated that the father had brought the kids to the fire station after the death of the mother with their most valued possessions. She stated that they had asked a neighbor to care for the cat, as they thought that he would be arrested and the children removed. She stated that the house was overly cleaned and amply stocked with food when she went in, like he was trying to prove he could care for them. She stated that the children must bath twice a day, as they were always very clean. She stated that the father offered much detail about everything, for example, telling her exactly how he spent a $100 donation. She stated that he told her he made 2 payments on the saxophone that he bought for Claire. She reported that the family did not continue with the church after the funeral and appeared to be very isolated. She stated that the children did well in school but did not appear to have any close friends.

"Collateral: ...stated that the father had brought the kids to the fire station after the death of the mother with their most valued possessions. She stated that they had asked a neighbor to care for the cat, as they thought that he would be arrested and the children removed. She stated that the house was overly cleaned and amply stocked with food when she went in, like he was trying to prove he could care for them. She stated that the children must bath twice a day, as they were always very clean. She stated that the

---

[36] When I spoke to the detective from the Sacramento County Sheriff's Office, after my father had been paroled, I asked about the situation where my father was brought into my interrogation room. I was told that there was nothing in the file that made any mention of that happening. However, the conversation wasn't really an interview but rather the gentleman kept making lengthy statements to which I could either affirm or deny. I had been a cop and was a licensed attorney at the time, so it was very clear to me that they weren't trying to gather any information but instead just wanted to make me go away.

father offered much detail about everything, for example, telling her exactly how he spent a $100 donation. She stated that he told her he made 2 payments on the saxophone that he bought for Claire. She reported that the family did not continue with the church after the funeral and appeared to be very isolated. She stated that the children did well in school but did not appear to have any close friends."
(Source: California Department of Health and Human Services, Child Protective Services)

Quite literally pointing to the shiny little distraction (the saxophone), my father could always make a showing that he was the best caregiver. In reality, we were one box of Sangria wine away from being in that apartment from which a strange smell was emanating and five corpses would later be discovered.

4 the children in the home for at least 12 hours after his wife, their mother died. The undersigned is
5 concerned that he did not call the authorities who could have offered medical assistance and possibly
6 tried to resuscitate their mother. The children were exposed to their mother's corpse for a number of
7 hours. The father proceeded to drink alcohol and panic. He talked about killing himself and
8 possible group suicide after the death of the mother. The children were exposed to a man who
9 appeared to have panicked and the children did not or were not able to call the authorities. The
10 undersigned also requests a psychological evaluation for the father to rule out obsessive compulsive disorder.
11
12 The undersigned is very concerned because not only did one child attempt suicide, but two children have attempted suicide since the death of their mother. This is a very closed family and at
13 one time, the undersigned was told that "if one of us goes down, we all go down."

"...the children in the home for at least 12 hours after his wife, their mother died. The undersigned is concerned that he did not call the authorities who could have offered medical assistance and possibly tried to resuscitate their mother. The children were exposed to their mother's corpse for a number of hours. The father proceeded to drink alcohol and panic. He talked about killing himself and possible group suicide after the death of the mother. The children were exposed to a man who appeared to have panicked and the children did not or were not able to call the authorities. The undersigned also requests a psychological evaluation for the father to rule out obsessive compulsive disorder.

The undersigned is very concerned because not only did one child attempt suicide, but two children have attempted suicide since the death of their mother. This is a very closed family and at one time, the undersigned was told that 'if one of us goes down, we all go down.'" (Source: California Department of Health and Human Services, Child Protective Services)

My father was not arrested or charged for my mother's death, and even after he admitted to child sexual abuse, he was allowed to roam the streets[37] for approximately a week. The following was

---

[37] Sadly, rape, molestation and similar offenses are not treated like a homicide would be wherein someone is immediately taken into custody and law enforcement, or the prosecutor, is trying to prevent bail. Instead, charges are referred for prosecution and the culprits are free to board a Greyhound bus to begin anew with a different victim. My question is, why? What happened with my father is not uncommon in today's society.

documented after we came into care but before the state decided to act against my father.

12 The father, Douglas Grieve, initially was residing in a homeless shelter affiliated with the
13 Salvation Army. He met with the undersigned on two occasions in which the undersigned provided
14 referrals to the appropriate community based organizations to assist the father in adhering to Court
15 ordered recommendations. Shortly after the communication with the father, a MDIC interview was
16 conducted with the eldest minor, ████████ This resulted in ████████ openly admitted that
17 her stepfather, Douglas Grieve, committed sexual molest and was quite explicit and descriptive in the
18 manner in which he abused her. Two days after the MDIC interview, Detective, ████ Dewante also
19 interviewed Douglas Grieve, with the Sheriff's department. During the interview, he provided
20 additional information that was quite descriptive, in which he admitted to sexually molesting the
21 minor, ████████ for a period of approximately five years. He admitted to having intercourse and
22 forcing the minor to have oral copulation with him. He was under the impression that he would serve
23 two days in jail, then be released to continue with his family reunification plan. However, Douglas
24 Grieve, was arrested approximately one week later and is currently awaiting sentencing at
25 Sacramento Main Jail. There, Douglas Grieve was offered services by Social Worker, ████

"The father, Douglas Grieve, initially was residing in a homeless shelter affiliated with the Salvation Army. He met with the undersigned on two occasions in which the undersigned provided referrals to the appropriate community based organizations to assist the father in adhering to Court ordered recommendations. Shortly after the communication with the father, a MDIC interview was conducted with the eldest minor...This resulted in...openly admitted that her stepfather, Douglas Grieve, committed sexual molest and was quite explicit and descriptive in the manner in which he abused her. Two days after the MDIC interview, Detective...Dewante also interviewed Douglas Grieve, with the Sheriff's department. During the interview, he provided additional information that was

100

quite descriptive, in which he admitted to sexually molesting the minor…for a period of approximately five years. He admitted to having intercourse and forcing the minor to have oral copulation with him. He was under the impression that he would serve two days in jail, then be released to continue with his family reunification plan. However, Douglas Grieve, was arrested approximately one week later and is currently awaiting sentencing at Sacramento Main Jail. There, Douglas Grieve was offered services by Social Worker…" (Source: California Department of Health and Human Services, Child Protective Services)

What about the homicide? Until the very end, it was believed that my mother was mentally unstable and delusional in thinking my father was trying to kill her. The prosecutor did not know there was a history of domestic violence or child abuse. If each individual episode (child abuse or domestic violence) is explained away, then no history of abuse or domestic violence is created. If we decide to pass on charges this time, a subsequent review will show no history, and a decision may be made to dismiss. Then next time, the past two incidents don't show up and the same thing could happen again. This happened to both claims of domestic violence and child abuse in our home. Nobody ever did anything, so there was never a history to support doing something with future incidents. Everyone just kept kicking the can.

John O'Meara, District Attorney's Office:

Mr. O'Meara reported this is a case that is not going to be prosecuted because it does not appear there was intent to kill the mother by restraining her. He reported at the time of the investigation, his

22

office was not aware of previous domestic violence or physical abuse toward the children. He reported it appears that the family did intend to restrain the mother to ensure that she would be present during the holidays and she died possibly from the position of the restraint. It appears that there was a period of time before authorities were notified because the family panicked and did not know what to do and thought they would all be arrested.

"<u>John O'Meara, District Attorney's Office</u>: Mr. O'Meara reported this is a case that is not going to be prosecuted because it does not appear there was intent to kill the mother by restraining her. He reported at the time of the investigation, his office was not aware of previous domestic violence or physical abuse toward the children. He reported it appears that the family did intend to restrain the mother to ensure that she would be present during the holidays and she died possibly from the position of the restraint. It appears that there was a period of time before authorities were notified because the family panicked and did not know what to do and thought they would all be arrested." (Source: California Department of Health and Human Services, Child Protective Services)

Curiosity may lead someone to consider the hammer incident but remember that was ruled a bizarre accident (can kicked again).

14 | Detective Jane Hall, Sacramento County Sheriff's Department:

15 | The undersigned spoke with Ms. Jane Hall regarding the incident where the mother was hit with

16 | a hammer by the father. Detective Hall reported she considered this domestic violence and was

17 | surprised when the District Attorney's Office did not follow up on this case. There was a report of

18 | domestic violence in which the father was threatening the mother with a hammer. He was swinging

19 | the hammer and it was reported that the mother stood up and got hit with the hammer in the head,

20 | and required four stitches. Please see attached police report, #98-051888.

"<u>Detective Jane Hall, Sacramento County Sheriff's Department</u>: The undersigned spoke with Ms. Jane Hall regarding the incident where the mother was hit with a hammer by the father. Detective Hall reported she considered this domestic violence and was surprised when the District Attorney's Office did not follow up on this case. There was a report of domestic violence in which the father was threatening the mother with a hammer. He was swinging the hammer and it was reported that the mother stood up and got hit with the hammer in the head, and required four stitches..." (Source: California Department of Health and Human Services, Child Protective Services)

My father admitted trying to scare his wife with a hammer, striking my mother and causing serious disfigurement requiring stitches. The reason cited for kicking the can: they didn't want kids in foster care (see excerpt in the previous chapter). These decisions would pave the way for a worsening condition and force my older sister to take on the role of my father's wife officially.

"When asked about her mother dying, ASHELY reported, 'It's all in the report. I don't want to talk about it anymore, please.' ASHLEY reported her mother was afraid her father would kill her, her mother, someday. He told her mother if anything happens to you 'CLAIRE will be my wife.' ASHLEY stated being confused because now CLAIRE sleeps in the same bed as her father sometimes.

When asked about sexual abuse regarding her sister, ASHLEY reported reluctantly that her father would in the last month, before they came into foster care, make CLAIRE sleep in the same bed with him. When her father would go to sleep, CLAIRE would come back into her own bed and he would come and get her and make her go back into the bedroom with him to sleep. ASHLEY clearly

104

did not feel comfortable talking about this. The undersigned stated we could come back to this topic at a later time. ASHLEY said, 'I'd really like that, I don't want to get my dad in trouble.' In a later conversation, ASHLEY reported she would ask her sister, CLAIRE, 'Why do you sleep with him?' and she replied, 'Because I have to. I'm afraid if I don't.' ASHLEY reported her sister, CLAIRE, had told her she did not want to sleep with her father, Mr. Grieve, but she is afraid that she might get hurt if she did not sleep with her father.

ASHLEY reported she wanted to live with her father, she stated he needs some help and needs to stop drinking, but she wants to live with him. ASHLEY reported, 'My father needs us. He needs us to help take care of him.'" (Source: California Department of Health and Human Services, Child Protective Services)

It would be months before the sexual abuse came to light. In the meantime, the signs were there, a history of allegations and all, but it would take too many resources to search for the information. Someone would have to check internal records, reach out to other agencies, contact collaterals, and conduct thorough interviews, which takes time. It's much easier to avoid following up on leads or gut feelings (intuition) by labeling something as bizarre, unusual, or odd.

21 | Detective Clark Fransher, Homicide Division :

22 | . Detective Fransher reported during his investigation he believes the family was all involved in

23 | the tying up and restraining of the mother and did not feel that this was a death from intent. He

24 | reported this was a very "unusual, odd case", but did not believe that any charges should be filed on

25 | these children or their father. It was reported by the detective that he did suspect sexual abuse by the

26 | father toward CLAIRE, although did not get any information that would substantiate this.

"Detective Clark Fransher, Homicide Division: Detective Fransher reported during his investigation he believes the family was all involved in tying up and restraining of the mother and did not feel that this was a death from intent. He reported this was a very 'unusual, odd case', but did not believe that any charges should be filed on these children or their father. It was reported by the detective that he did suspect sexual abuse by the father toward CLAIRE, although did not get any information that would substantiate this." (Source: California Department of Health and Human Services, Child Protective Services)

While it is not easy to conceal my anger, at least in this chapter, investigating abuse, neglect, and domestic violence is brutally difficult for a myriad of reasons. Barriers include uncooperative or vulnerable witnesses, lack of resources and time, high staff turnover, lack of communication or miscommunication between agencies, and elusive evidence. While interning for the Circuit Attorney's Office, a prosecutor addressed the jury and said something to the effect of, "Domestic violence does not happen on the 50-yard line at the Super Bowl in front of millions and millions of people." I would add, "It happens in the booth, in the back, in the

106

corner, in the dark,"[38] away from prying eyes. However, in my family's case, there were independent incidents where the facts did not lead to the conclusions reached. It almost seemed that investigations were conducted to support a decision rather than leading to a conclusion. Giving the investigators every benefit screams training to me, but it can also be from overworked practitioners consumed in thought concerning other matters instead of being focused during a given investigation. Then, when taking a closer look, my records show there was an extensive history painting an entirely different picture from the individual entries. The multiple failures to intervene led to escalating violence and loss of life.

As an attorney, I have seen firsthand why I did not get removed from my violent home after my mother's death, and conditions continued to deteriorate. Sadly, I feel we do not value the lives of children as we should and therefore underfund the social services agencies tasked with protecting the vulnerable. There are too many cases like mine for the system to deal with, so it is often easier to go for the low-hanging fruit and move on to the next case. My question is: why were the records destroyed so soon after my mother's death? There is no statute of limitations for homicide, but it is difficult to proceed with a case if all the records have been destroyed.

---

[38] I got this from a Flip Wilson show. We did not grow up watching contemporary shows, which added a layer to our isolation.

DOJ Report Destruction
Verification Form

DEC 19 2003

(signature)

DOJ report destroyed by: Date destroyed:

CS35

Birth 19 Jan 1961
Death 6 Dec 1998 (aged 37)
Rancho Cordova, Sacramento County, California, USA
Burial Camellia Memorial Lawn Cemetery
Plot Shrine of Rest Mausoleum, North Niches, Tier F, Niche 2
Memorial ID - 167306814

Let her death lead to lives saved. These things still occur, but people are getting more competent at concealing them. Let's get better at investigating them, protecting those harmed, and holding abusers responsible. This is our job—our duty— even as community members.

        *   *   *

My father kept a parakeet in a cage. It flew away one day. I know I was around six or seven years old because CNN was talking about Desert Storm on the news. We had been left at home while my

108

father had gone grocery shopping. At some point, I opened the cage. I do not recall if it was to try to pet the parakeet or what, but the bird got out of the cage. We could not get the bird back in the cage before my father came home. It was just our luck that the parakeet flew out when he opened the door. I do not even remember what type of beating I got, but how could I not? Just a fleeting memory, but as I reflect, I think it is interesting that of all the creatures my father could get, he chose one that could soar above everyone and everything and fly away—one he decided to keep caged.

Much like all of us, eventually, the bird escaped. It was just a little parakeet. A few hours later, the weather changed. Dark clouds rolled in, and a menacing storm formed. I hope the parakeet survived. But even if it didn't, I am sure the few hours of freedom it acquired were better than an entire life caged under my father's roof. If only my mother could have flown away. Surely, she was given wings.

Chapter 9

Let Me Show You

(let mee shoh yoo)

"If you give a man a fish, you feed him for a day. If you teach a man..." wait, what are we teaching?

I must reiterate the exercise of self-care as I share my childhood experiences. After my mother's death, life did not change much—at least not for the better. We went to school as if my mother's death was normal. I started getting into more trouble at school and was suspended multiple times.

One time, when I was suspended from middle school, my father brought me into the room now belonging to my older sister and him. He tried to teach me a lesson that I often repress, but it always resurfaces with a mixture of paralyzing negative emotions. The door was open, bed made. My sisters were likely at school. On this day, I believe he told me my paternal grandmother taught him about sex through a hands-on demonstration. I was crying, not from being physically hurt, but for fear of what would come. Not an all-out bawling, but rather a mournful weeping and quiet appreciation that something will forever change. Something was about to happen that was not right at the hands of my father—a caregiver in my life to whom I should be able to turn for support.

That day, I knew that I could not fight my father. He was a full-grown man with military experience. He had exercised power and control[39] over me countless times, so there was no need for a show of force today—my mother's absence said it all. Nobody was coming to my aid, no concerned school employees, no well-intentioned bubbly

---

[39] I still cannot simply disclose this. I must outline defenses and justification to lessen the guilt I feel for being violated.

social workers with empty promises, and certainly no law enforcement who had better things to do. Everyone in my family feared him. Our world was isolated and lonely, cloaked in dark and suffocating garments of intimate violence and emotional hostility. I should be grateful he permitted me to breathe that day. My life was in his hands, and he could have ended it on a whim. As a skinny[40] little runt, barely weighing eighty pounds, I mistakenly believed this was how life was supposed to be.

I knew what was to transpire—just not how it could be prevented. It would be something sexual. One drunken night, my father woke me up, forced me to go to their bedroom, and made me sit on the floor against the wall, facing their king-sized bed. It was dark, but I could make out my mother dutifully lying naked in compliance. He had his way with her as she lay motionless. I witnessed and heard it all. When it was over, I was allowed to go to bed. Although this was unusual, it was not particularly shocking. He had had sex with my older sister[41] while I was lying in the same hotel room

---

[40] Most guys will not admit they are vulnerable or defenseless. Isn't that the opposite of masculinity? Just another reason to avoid disclosing. It took years for me to open up about what happened to me; I generally just talked about what happened to my mother or older sister.

[41] I learned in early 2023 that banging my head on my pillow to go to sleep was a common coping modality; many years after doing it as a child. As a child, I used to do it unintentionally and it would keep my sisters awake since we shared a room. To avoid getting in trouble when they complained, I used to stay awake until my sisters fell asleep before banging my head. This is when I started seeing my father come into the room and crawl into bed with my sister. On those nights, I had to wait until he was done, sounds and

bed (we, on several occasions, took the little cash we had and hid in a hotel to elude police when my mother escaped). He kicked me out of the bottom bunk of the bunk bed shared by my younger sister and me numerous times to masturbate on the sheets. I guess, for whatever reason, on those nights, he was not having sex with my older sister. Then, of course, all those times, he had sex with my older sister while I pretended to sleep. So, I knew what was to transpire was sexual.

He pulled down my pants and made me lie down on my back at the foot of the bed. My legs hung over the edge, bent at the knee. I looked up at the ceiling of the apartment.[42] I felt his mustache below and heard the sounds his mouth was making. This was not like the beatings to which I was accustomed. What am I supposed to do in this situation? To whom do I turn? I was at a loss for any way to process what was happening; even today, it is something I cannot comprehend. How do you do this to your child? When he finished, he pulled down his pants. He lay beside me at the foot of the bed—his hairy legs hanging over the edge bent at the knee. He told me to do as he had just demonstrated.

I did not want to—I froze, still weeping. If I did not comply, would he beat me? I did not want to

---

all. Again, on occasion, he would kick me out of my bed. I still have trouble falling asleep and staying asleep.

[42] I generally try to avoid listening to or reading other survivor stories because I already must deal with my own. However, I do come across the lessons learned from other presenters. I don't know her name, but another survivor said interview rooms should not have white walls because she had to stare at a white ceiling when she was sexually abused.

get hit but what he wanted me to do was gross, like really awful. This is one of those moments where I look back and am grateful for my life because things could have been so much worse. Many have endured far worse than I have and must find the strength to face each day. If things had worsened, I could not continue living because I was already so close to the edge. After a few minutes of my defiance, he told me to lay on top of him, unclothed, belly to belly. This was just weird, but I was not bleeding or anything from being beaten like a normal punishment. I was still crying but not in physical pain. I tried not to cry on him and get him mad. We sat there for a couple of moments that felt like an eternity. He then told me to leave. No beating—I got lucky, or did I?

Please understand when I say a part of me is not okay. You can try to lock it up and suppress it, which will sometimes work, but it will always come back. You cannot choose the time and place that the memories will resurface. You can read a work email, buy groceries at the store, or spend time with your family when the memory resurfaces. Especially considering the latter, what do you do? "Hey guys, guess what I just thought about?" My only answer is prevention: stop the situations that create the memories because I have not identified a method to thoroughly purge these memories from my mind, except perhaps suicide. I am not advocating suicide (I do not believe that is the answer), but I have often told myself suicide is a permanent solution to erase memories. This is not healthy, so my life is filled with footings[43] that stave off thoughts of suicide (this, I believe, is the best answer).

Beyond something merely happening to me, I must also address the potential there was for me to become my father. A parent teaches their child right and wrong. My father was trying to show me that incest was okay through grooming. In essence, grooming attempts to normalize inappropriate sexual conduct with a child and prepare them for engaging in such behavior. My father told me it happened to him; then he showed me how it is done and tried to give me a turn. As a child, how was I to know that what he was trying to teach me was wrong if this was all I learned on the subject?

One memory will always haunt me of what could have been. On occasion, I was left at home with my younger sister. I used to hate it because she did not listen and I would get into trouble for something she caused. Sometimes, I would also get into mischief with her, but the result was the same. I remember once, when I was in elementary school, we tried to make dessert. We took a cup of water and poured in sugar and other random dessert-like spices. We spilled some and were supposed to clean it up. I cannot recall what the punishment was, or even if we got caught, but this is the type of thing that inevitably led to a beating. I probably use the word beating too often, but it was never a slap on the wrist. It was always some

---

[43] I discuss this concept more in Chapter 11. For now, most practitioners should be familiar with anchors—I learned through trauma informed care training.

horrific whipping with a belt, extension cord, or other more painful objects, often accompanied by additional creative punishments.

My parents' version of morality was beaten into us, including my father's condonation of incestuous behavior. The memory that haunts me is a moment at a crossroads of which I was unaware. One of the times I was left at home with Ashley, I was wrestling her.

Before I go on, let me add the following. Claire's story is hers to share, but there is a very relevant point about the prevalence of sexual misconduct in the home. On at least two occasions, my mother cleaned and dressed Claire and presented her to my father for sex. On those occasions, my mother chose to stay home and not flee. My sister does not blame[44] my mother because of the totality of circumstances, but it does add another layer.

Returning to my younger sister and me, our tussling ended with me landing on top of her while lying on the ground. For a moment, we sat there, and then she said, "Get off." I did, and we continued playing. As I reflect, so many different things could have happened, which would have occurred at least in part because my father taught me. How am I so lucky to have rejected these teachings? Although only a split second, it could have forever changed my sister's life and my own.

---

[44] When one is in a domestic violence relationship, they are coerced to do things against their better judgment. Those very acts are part of the control tactics because the survivor feels guilt for their actions or inaction, further preventing disclosure. I am not saying this is okay, but having walked in those shoes, I understand and know it is hard to accept that the original blame lies with the abuser.

Increasing awareness is just one more reason sharing is so important. Who was in my home to tell me what my father was doing was wrong? Who was present to say what both of my parents allowed was unlawful? On the contrary, it seemed that the authorities endorsed all these acts because they did nothing to stop it.

When I was reviewing the Child Protective Services records, I came across the statement from the vice principal at my middle school. I had been making some inappropriate sexual remarks[45] at school, and he had noted that this was a red flag. He told the investigator that he would keep a closer eye on me. I wish he did more than keep an eye on me at school. The harm occurred at home.

We did not know what was happening was wrong. The physical abuse seemed wrong because we were told to lie. Lying is bad, so what we lied about must be wrong. For the sexual stuff, there was no discussion, so there were no lies. Even sexual education in school, to which my father was vehemently opposed, did not inform us that parents should not have sex with their children. How could we know?

I know of a lady who did not realize until college her father was lying when he justified his molestation by saying it's a father's job to prepare a daughter for their husband through demonstrative acts. As a college student, her father was still forcefully engaging in sex with her.

My older sister began speaking to people about the sexual abuse, understanding it was wrong, but

---

[45] See excerpt in Chapter 1, page 10.

she was not believed. We barely spoke for years after eventually being removed from our home, and when we did speak, I did not want to discuss our childhood. So, it was not until I was thirty-five when I learned my mother presented Claire to my father for sex, and I was thirty-eight when I spoke to Ashley about her recollection[46] or experience with this form of abuse. Disclosure takes time.

As an attorney, I had a case with a sibling group with tons of horrible sexual and other abuse allegations. The state, I believe, brought kids in and out of care for neglect and other issues but nothing on sexual abuse. The Guardian ad Litem had a genogram of the family, and many relatives were victims of or perpetrated sexual abuse (including at least one grandfather incarcerated for rape). While the kids were in state custody, the prosecutor courageously filed charges based on the allegations. It was in the town newspaper—shocking the community.

About thirty days later, one little girl in the family asked to talk to her foster mother. The foster mother recounts a conversation lasting about thirty minutes where the little girl wanted to know what was happening with her father, how long he would be in jail, and what would happen to her. After the foster mother explained all this, disclosures started pouring out of this poor child. The foster mother, well-appraised of all the allegations, immediately contacted the social worker for a forensic interview.

---

[46] It was hard to bring this up because I suspected nothing happened with Ashley, but I did not want to imply she suffered less if she was not sexually abused.

A brief commercial on forensic interviews: it is so hard to talk about this stuff, and now we have a child who has already started to disclose to someone. If that child has to make a disclosure to a social worker, who contacts law enforcement (asking their own questions of the child), and then potentially to a juvenile officer, we are setting the case up for legal failure. Once we have a child who we believe will make a disclosure, there should be a forensic interview. This is an interview by a trained expert in a safe location[47] who is the only one asking questions. The prosecutor, social worker, state attorney, and law enforcement can be in another room, watching through a camera. Human trafficking cases may even have individuals from the federal government in addition to state and local officials. Before terminating the interview, the interviewer will check in with the other disciplinary team members to see if follow-up questions need to be asked. The interviewer briefly resumes questioning, utilizing the rapport established with the child. Otherwise, if a child is forced to make a disclosure five or six times, they are mentally and physically exhausted by the time we get them in for the forensic interview to make an official recorded statement.

If I had disclosed, I would have told them to ask one of the other people to whom I spoke.

---

[47] I witnessed firsthand the difficult financial decisions that had to be made by an organization providing emergency shelter for children and forensic interviews. There are not enough service providers, and working for an agency that cannot guarantee a paycheck is challenging, adding to unavailability.

Furthermore, the suspect or alleged perpetrator has constitutionally protected rights; they get an attorney. There is a chance that every time a child disclosed, they provided different details, not necessarily conflicting. However, a reasonable attorney may paint those various statements as being inconsistent and suggest the child is lying. Laws across the states are inconsistent in this area, but in many cases, a child victim may have to take the stand in a court of law and be cross-examined. Even if that's not the case, we don't need to give the defense unnecessary reasons to weaken our case. I have nothing against the defense; they are merely doing their job—required for a fair imbalanced system—but we do not need to create distractions.

So, the awesome foster mother brought in this little girl for a forensic interview, and I attended as the state attorney since I was on this case. The tender little girl disclosed that it (the sexual abuse) started when she was in first grade and used to sleep on a couch in the living room. Her father came to her at night and started molesting her with his hands. What bothered her the most was that she would be tired for school the next[48] day.

---

[48] I debated adding this but ultimately decided most bad actors would not turn to my book for self-help. Unfortunately, marital strife has led to children making false disclosures. A truthful disclosure, especially in a younger child, may not be in chronological order, could have gaps or confusing aspects, and likely will not emphasize facts essential to proving legal elements (what the child feels is important may not carry as much weight with practitioners). However, nice, neat, orderly disclosures, matching my legal elements, and potentially

Grooming essentially isolates a prospective victim, builds a relationship with them, and normalizes inappropriate sexual conduct. The sexually inappropriate behavior did not impact this child as much as being tired for school. Consider the idea of tickling a child. Sexual acts in appropriate circumstances are pleasurable and enjoyable, as tickling is for a young child. Grooming a young child can make these sexually abusive acts analogous to tickling, adding to a child's inability[49] to identify these acts as wrong. A child may not identify this as a "bad touch."

For all of these reasons, I maintain that I am lucky. Some parents try to teach their kids how to play sports; their kids just don't get it. Other parents try to teach their child a trade, like plumbing or carpentry, but their child doesn't understand. My parents tried to teach us something more atrocious, but it didn't stick. I thank God I did not learn this trade.

---

using terminology that is not age appropriate always cause me to pause.

[49] This child did not die. Yet they must live with what was done to them. When we focus on reducing the number of kids in foster care per thousand instead of improving training, what happened to this child may not have been discovered. Justifying an emphasis on numerically reducing kids in care based on child fatalities ignores the impact abuse has on a child who lives and how it negatively affects them moving forward. Improving training can lead to fewer kids in care because we can better determine the appropriate response instead of a mandate to reduce headcount and focus on purely preventative services. The means to an objective cannot be underestimated.

Chapter 10

Surviving State Custody

(ser-vahyv-ing steyt kuhs-tuh-dee)

"... and now you know the rest of the story."[50]

---

[50] Paul Harvey. I grew up in the original Twilight Zone (watching television and living in an environment foreign to my peers).

Cases like mine are still occurring, perhaps with more alarming frequency, because our society[51] is allowing it. We are accountable for the people we elect and the resulting decisions, such as whether or not to fund child welfare or mental health services. Without good leadership and sufficient resources, cost-saving measures will allow vulnerable people—such as children—to be harmed.

As a practitioner, I often get upset at the term "baby snatcher" because of how difficult and infrequent those snatches occur. Before writing this, I spoke with the director of a child welfare agency, pushing to reduce the number of kids in care and entering care (consistent with a national trend). This director had the best intentions and was metaphorically playing with a deck missing too many cards. I also agree that, at times, a child is removed when other resolutions are more appropriate; however, some of the most egregious cases occur where multiple opportunities to intervene are missed. The director argued that in their decades-long tenure in this field, they could count the number of cases I described on a single hand (I wonder how many they missed).

---

[51] On January 17, 2023, an elected representative asked in an open hearing about the economic benefits of the death of abused children, saying the quiet part out loud. He was purely talking dollars, as the director I spoke to was discussing numbers. This view fails to promote intervention and prevention of child abuse, neglect, and domestic violence. It falls on society's shoulders to decide if these are the types of decisions we want to make. Human life has no value if we take it out of the equation.

Especially considering inadequate training, victims can see if someone is just trying to check the boxes—looking for a way to close the case and move on. If the emphasis is reducing the number of kids in care (wholly focused on the number of foster kids per 1,000 citizens) instead of better investigatory training, how will children feel safe disclosing what they are going through? I would not have trusted that sharing what was truthfully happening would have rescued me from the abuse. The director stated that research shows child fatality does not increase in jurisdictions with far lower rates of children in care per 1,000. What about the kids who do not die? Do we care about them? While this may drive down numbers on paper, will it numerically make more children safe? The ultimate claim was that there would be more efficient resource use if the system dealt with fewer[52] kids. But if we fail to intervene because we are blind to what's occurring, how do we break the cycle and prevent future generational harm? This will result in higher future numbers. This director was trying to provide more preventative services and let families be families, which is a good goal. However, what if we do not clearly understand what is happening and try to slap a Band-Aid on that? We will put a Band-Aid on a knee and miss

---

[52] Maybe that's also what the DA thought after my father hit my mother in the head with a hammer and decided we should not go into foster care. No child fatality, but an adult fatality and a child who attempted homicide.

addressing a concussion[53] (far more often than we know).

I believe the focus should be on better training (which necessarily means workers shouldn't have to take phone calls and handle reports during training) and ensuring sufficient staffing to take the necessary time to determine what is transpiring—including contacting peers, more collaterals, and other agencies—so appropriate steps can be taken.

So, what was enough for my siblings and me to come into care? Clearly, not a homicide. What finally started the process for us was an attempted homicide, followed by a suicide attempt, on top of my mother's death and years of domestic violence and child abuse, occurring and documented across multiple[54] years and agencies. It happened after forcing a child to feel the only way to stay safe and to shield her siblings from harm was an unspeakable act that is difficult to live with. But my sister is not a child fatality statistic, even though she has wished so often that she was. It happened because a system that avoided bringing kids into care failed to adequately train investigators and provide proper resources and support to achieve its mandates effectively.

My older sister did a single act to protect Ashley and me that fulfilled a lifetime's worth of expectations any person could ever have of an

---

[53] Ideally, we will improve as a system by identifying and addressing the root causes instead of being reactionary.

[54] Imagine a database shared by the various entities, pooling information, and using an AI algorithm that helps identify patterns. We have the ability to do this right now, but we don't because of a lack of resource allocation.

older sibling. Conditions deteriorated to the point where the only plausible option Claire saw to keep us safe was to kill my father. She was around fifteen years old when she devised and proceeded to carry out a plan to kill him. There was an altercation in which Claire broke his foot and was winning against him. She was strangling him, and his struggle to fight was waning. His face turned purple, and future safety was at hand—Claire was succeeding. Then, Ashley, who was about eleven years old, stopped Claire. It took so much for Claire to get to the point where killing another human seemed the only option to stop the sexual, physical, and emotional abuse and to prevent another death. Then, to take the next step of trying to kill a human,[55] only to be stopped by someone she was trying to protect. Claire was devastated and without hope. Ashley foiled her near-complete attempt to protect us. If you reached this point in the book, what other option was there? What is the right thing to do if 911 never helps and instead causes further harm? Shortly afterward, Claire attempted suicide.

The documentation shows Ashley and I found Claire during her attempt, but I do not recall this event. My father tried to remove the belt around Claire's neck as she hung herself in the bedroom closet but was having difficulties getting her loose. So, he called 911, but he was able to remove the belt before they arrived and therefore hung up the phone. Police still responded because it was a 911

---

[55] Calling my father human is difficult but if I do not, how am I any better?

hang-up. Claire was removed and placed in a mental institution. While there, she came clean about what had been transpiring at home, and apparently, they finally believed her. It was as if nobody had ever taken a moment to review our entire history, but through this ordeal, someone's attention was grabbed, and they saw the big picture. Days after Claire's disclosure, Ashley and I were finally removed from this nightmare, only to start a new life in a broken system, forever separated from one another[56] in different cities. An entirely different battle began once I was in state custody.

Shortly after I became an attorney, when giving a motivational speech to a group of older youth, I asked permission to embellish how I came into care. I gave the following speech:[57]

> I will never forget when I was in eighth-grade physical education class and was removed. I was attending Mill's Middle School, out on the blacktop. You may not believe this, considering the brawny masculine physique that stands before you today, but I was not always this way. I didn't always look like the Rock. I was a skinny little runt. Physical education was not one of my favorite classes. I was not the last one picked; teams would

---

[56] It is difficult to find placements for sibling groups, minorities, and teenagers—we checked all three boxes.

[57] Life will be "life," but you can choose to see things positively; focus on what is possible instead of what did not work out. There is nothing to lose by putting a positive spin on things and avoiding dwelling on the negative. I no longer had to worry about staying alive!

rather play a person short. Plus, I did not fit in.

I'll digress momentarily. When you are sheltered as I was, things that come naturally for some and are taken for granted by others are foreign to us. Social interactions have always been complex for me; it is like I'm watching myself act as if I'm playing a role. Although I have improved on this front, I'm uncomfortable being thanked or congratulated. It is not something I was used to. For us, there are so many hurdles we must face, known and unknown, but we must do just that. We must be cognizant of the hurdles we face and conquer them—including social interactions. We must find a way to move forward.

Commercial over. Back at Mills Middle School, physical education class, eighth-grade. I'm thirteen and not yet the Rock. There must have been like seven county sheriffs that pulled onto the blacktop from every direction. If you'll indulge my embellishments a little, there were swat teams repelling from helicopters. Well, maybe no helicopters, but all that law enforcement[58] was there for me. The other students probably thought the strange quiet kid was a criminal mastermind. It was

---

[58] It was like the system was making up for years of missed opportunities.

awesome! That was the day I entered "the system."

Truthfully, I don't know why there were three Sacramento County Sheriff's cars that day, but other than that and the part about my masculine physique, the rest is accurate.

Instead of being placed in a foster home with my siblings, we were split up and sent to different cities. As an attorney, I always stressed the importance of keeping sibling groups together and obtaining sibling bond assessments[59] if keeping the group together was impossible. Our relationships would be, and still are, to a degree, strained enough with our shared experiences. The distance in growing up for the rest of our childhood only added to our barriers.

I was not lucky enough to be placed in a foster home. I went from an environment where I had no "real" family to an environment where I had "no" family. I would spend two and a half years in a group home filled with higher-risk youth, individuals with criminal, gang, or mentally unstable backgrounds. Like in the movies, when someone goes to prison, I felt the need to assert myself. Sadly, I didn't have the build to go with it. I got into an altercation. There was an older teen there named Larry. He was a gang member. We were in the recreation room of a three-bedroom house. The social

---

[59] We need more for the record than "the kids aren't safe together." However, we need help from society because there are never enough placement providers.

worker was meeting with the group home manager about my placement when I accidentally stepped on Larry's shoe. He told me to step on his foot again. I knew well what sarcasm meant (my father drove home the point with a screwdriver). I looked at Larry and I looked down the hallway to the meeting. The office was down the hall, past a few rooms, and to the left. I looked at Larry again, who was larger than I and more muscular. He also seemed inquisitively upset. I looked down the hall again and liked my odds.

I stomped on his foot while pivoting into a sprint stance. I took off down the hallway and then took flight. About halfway down the hall, my feet were no longer on the ground, and my arms flailed in slow motion like an action hero escaping a Hollywood explosion. Bam! It all abruptly stopped as I crashed into the wall, shy of turning left. Larry caught up to me and shoved me down the rest of the hallway, face-first into the wall. Oops. The manager came roaring out of the office, yelling and screaming at me for creating an altercation as soon as I had walked through the door. Larry had my back from that day forward, and the manager had my heart. She treated me like a human being, tough love and all, but would do things like take me shopping on her day off. Life would not be without struggles, but it was far better than the home from which I came.

You wouldn't know this was a group home except for seeing people entering and exiting the house. Sure, many different cars parked in front of the house as staff would come and go, and we had the quintessential group home van parked in the garage, but we were mostly made to stay inside. I was familiar with isolation.[60] Despite facing new challenges with which any youth would struggle, I still had a lot to work through. As an example of a new challenge, the following handwritten entry requires some background details.

At age fifteen, I was working in a program and had money. I would buy things. Our teenager allowance was a couple of bucks a week and thirty dollars a month for clothing, which would all be taken away if we got into trouble. We were always in trouble. Having a job, which most did not, meant I had things others did not. I had a rule that I would not lend out more than two items at a time until I got something back. This one kid did not like that rule.

---

[60] As a parent knowing isolation, it is a struggle finding a safety balance in allowing a teenager to socialize sufficiently especially during covid. Only the future knows if I struck the right balance.

Sherman Group Inc.
Incident Report

Date: 10/2/00   Time: 8:40 am/pm Report #_____   Facility: Greenwich
Location:_____

Youth Involved
Name: Matthew_____ DOB: 6/14/84 DOP: 8/31/00 M/F M
      Albert_____

Staff
Involved: Tayna

Type of Incident
✓ AWOL ____ Medical ✓ Injury ____ Self Abuse ____ Assault to staff
____ ✓ Assault to youth ____ Property Damage ____ Restraint Type____
____ Contraband Other:____

Description of Incident: The incident occurred when Albert came to staff
and said Matthew had punched him. I then asked Matthew, who insisted
that he did not. I called Albert to the front of the house, due to
him being in his room to prevent an earlier confrontation. Albert
wanted his things back that Matthew had borrowed. Matthew refused.
I asked Albert in front of Matthew whether or not he hit him he
said Yes. Albert then went back to his room and shut the door.
Matthew became enraged, threw the plastic cup in his hand shattering
it on the counter, he then threw one of the dinning room chairs
to the floor. He took off down the hallway saying "I hit him,
I'm going to hit him alright. He had reached Albert's door
and found that Albert had blocked it. He proceded to kick cont....

Immediate Action taken(include persons contacted, Advice received, please also include report #
and Badge # if Law Enforcement was called) Including disciplinary (when appropriate). I called
the Senior then called 911 due to the state of mind Matthew was in.
I also called A-parkway to let them know that Albert was probably on his
Follow-up Action: when the officers arrived a missing persons report
was done. Then I made the necessary calls to his S.W. and
mom.
Persons to notify of incident and follow-up action

P.O./Social Worker Nick Pulido_____ Date 10/2/00 Time 8:44
Police/Sheriff D. Johnson / Williams_____ Date 10/2/00 Time 8:51
Beeper Person Cherie Holland (Senior) Date 10/2/00 Time 8:50

Community Care Licensing Notified Yes_____ No_____
Name of licensing Analyst_____ Faxed: Yes____ No____

_____ 10/2/00
Staff Reporting   Date

_____ 10/3/00
Residential Director SR. Manager   Date

The door. Eventually kicking it off the hinges. He then jumped on Albert's bed &
Albert was doing his homework and started punching him. I grabbed Matthew
by the shirt, then by the waist. He then broke lose and caught Albert again this
time it was on Christians bed. Again he started to punch Albert. I got
Matthew around his neck with one arm and pulled him towards me. This gave
Albert room to get up and out of the room. When he preceded to still
go after Albert I again grabbed pulled his shirt. His shirt (Kings Jersey)
ripped apart. He kicked Alberts file cabinet and ran out of the room
looking for Albert again. Noticing that Albert was outside the house
Matthew took off chasing Albert up the street. Because I could not
leave the house due to other youths being at home, I asked one of the
other youths to assist me. I asked him to go after Matthew. Due to
the state of mind he was in I did not want Matthew to catch up to
Albert and do any more harm to him. Both Matthew and Shawn
returned. Matthew went in his room, while I was checking out the damage
to Alberts room he packed some clothes and left.

In regards to the earlier confrontation when Albert asked for his
Channel locks (to do weights) Matthew threw them towards Albert hitting
the frame to the door.

In case it is difficult to read, this kid (Matthew) kicked my solid core door off the hinges and attacked me because I refused to loan him a tool for lifting weights until something else of mine was returned. Staff could not control him or prevent him from attacking me, even when staff grabbed him around the neck. I fled the house and he went outside searching to no avail. He later ran away and I returned.

This wasn't the only battle I had. The following is an excerpt from early on in my placement showing the internal turmoil I was still processing.

Axis V
(Circle) ① 2 3 4 5 6 7 8 9 0 (no change)   Secondary Axis II

Axis IV   Current GAF: 60

Past Year GAF: 60

Summary

* Types and focus of therapy / rehabilitation to be provided
* Coordination with other providers / programs
* Additional Information

Albert continues to live in the group home to which he was sent after being removed from his father's care in April of 1999. His mood and behavior have improved, but significant periods of depression sometimes overtake him and this can result in his feeling suicidal. Just recently the staff at his group home found him in bed with a belt wrapped around his neck. Albert explained that he was disturbed at being isolated from family, feeling alone, and had been told that if you wrap a belt around your neck it will tighten and strangle you during the night. It is these depressive feelings, and a tendency to frequently aggravate other which in turn creates social isolation, that are problematic for Albert. This is a very likable youngster who is bright and shows remarkable tenacity. Despite the tragic losses he has had over the past year he continues to strive to succeed in school and looks forward to entering college. Although relationships are often problematic for Albert, he has the capacity to be engaging and perceptive. Nevertheless, Albert has difficulty experiencing strong distressing emotions that are appropriate for the situation he finds himself in. Instead he wrestles with his thoughts and feelings in private, then failing to resolve the difficulty, becomes saddened and suicidal. At other times he simply misbehaves.

I read the last sentence to mean the following: on top of all this trauma, Albert was still a teenager.

Chapter 11

Help Yourself

(help yər'self)

If you find within yourself value worth investing in, others will too.

I became accustomed to residing in a group home. Staff came and left, but I remained year after year. It wasn't perfect, but I knew how to work the system. That was the case until they decided I should move on. I started getting into trouble with some of the youth and the group home threatened to send me to a higher-level facility— the path to California Youth Authority. I knew I was capable of achieving more. I worked the program and checked the boxes until I could go into foster care (my original destination that was never available—most placements do not want teenagers). The result was that I lived in three different homes in three separate towns and attended three dissimilar high schools during my sophomore year.

I need to pause to discuss my second placement or first foster home. I think there was too great of an emphasis on my designated race and placing me accordingly. I grew up in a mixed-race household and then lived in a mixed group home. I was used to dysfunction. I also did not grow up in a religious[61] household, nor was any home I lived in affluent. My first foster home was all black. I spent every Sunday going from church to church, and the family was very involved in youth football. Did they know anything about me? I did not fit in. I felt like a dog they had to take with them everyplace because kennels would not accept me. For these and other reasons, it was decided by all that this

---

[61] My mother was very religious, and my father was an atheist. My father lives and my mother does not... I have struggled with religion, but God's impact continues to grow in my life, displacing my negative history.

was not a suitable placement. Every blown placement for a child creates barriers to new placements. I was that used car with multiple owners now, that Carfax cautions against. The last home I was placed in was a perfect environment, and I tried to make up for all the years of living I had missed.

<blockquote>
6 Albert stated that he appreciates being placed in a biracial home. His biological

7 father is Caucasian and his mother is African American. The foster father is African American and

8 has a large extended interracial family. Therefore, Albert feels comfortable and enjoys the company

9 of family members who come often to visit. The foster father and Albert have a good relationship

10 because according to Albert, they like the same things, music, computers, and food. The foster

11
12 father enjoys having Albert in his home because he feels Albert is a good role model for his younger

13 foster sibling. Likewise, the foster father has also been a positive influence on Albert by assisting

14 him to develop positive relationships with others and by encouraging Albert to do well in school.

15 Albert has also adjusted well to his new school and community. He continues to

16 maintain a high grade point average and participates in recreational and church activities.
</blockquote>

"Albert stated that he appreciates being placed in a biracial home. His biological father is Caucasian and his mother is African American. The foster father is African American and has a large extended interracial family. Therefore, Albert feels comfortable and enjoys the company of family members who come often to visit. The foster father and Albert have a good relationship because according to Albert, they like the same things, music, computers, and food. The foster father enjoys having Albert in his home because he feels Albert is a good role model for his younger foster sibling. Likewise, the foster father has also been a positive influence on Albert by assisting him to develop positive relationships with others and by encouraging Albert to do well in school.

Albert has also adjusted well to his new school and community. He continues to maintain a high-grade point average and participates in recreational and church activities." (Source: California Department of Health and Human Services, Child Protective Services)

A point of clarification: I had a lot in common with my foster father's son and his significant other at the time, Sandra. Sandra still holds an important place in my life and we catch up often. They functioned as my foster parents, but on paper, my foster father was a Korean War veteran in his seventies. His wife had passed away but had the primary role in fostering. It was a dysfunctional placement in which I thrived. The following is a letter of recommendation on my behalf. I often forget about the electric vehicle.

LETTER OF RECOMMENDATION

It gives me great pleasure to write this letter on behalf of Mr. Albert Grieve. I have known Albert now for about three years. During this time I have been able to observe the academic progress and maturing of a wonderful and remarkable young man.

Albert possesses the qualities common to all outstanding students. He has an excellent work ethic, and is not satisfied until his work has met his own high standards, however difficult a task might be. His attendance is impeccable and he never fails to complete an assignment. What makes Albert unique is his background. Presently, Albert lives in a foster home. He has had a difficult upbringing, to say the least. His mother is deceased, and his father is in prison. Along the way he was separated from his two sisters, who reside in separate foster homes. In this time Albert has bounced around to several schools. It's these difficult circumstances, which make Albert's individual achievements as unlikely as they are impressive.

From the first day I was introduced to Albert, midway through his tenth grade year, I was impressed. While he had every excuse to fail in school and in life, Albert used his adversity as a motivating tool. From the beginning he has consistently set goals, and focused on getting the best grades possible. He has and unstoppable drive and determination, which I have seldom seen even in students that have grown up under the best of circumstances. Since he has been at Laguna, his grades have been excellent.

Other students like as well as respect Albert for his personal ideals as well as his intellectual achievements. He is consistently looked to for guidance and leadership in the classroom. I have personally seen Albert take command of situations that flounder about and motivate the entire group with his firm leadership through the final goal. Other teachers speak very highly of Albert. He is extremely polite, and respectful; traits which should not be taken lightly considering your average teenager of his generation.

Albert's list of extra curricular activities is extensive. He has turned himself into an excellent wrestler. He joined the team when he came here, and has worked extremely hard to make the varsity squad. Albert has also been heavily involved in campus life, participating in several clubs and being seen at many school events. He is also a member of the nationally recognized school newspaper, and has elevated himself to editor status. He also created a remarkable senior project. He built a full scale operational, electric car. It was quite a sight to see him driving around campus.

During my association with Albert I have come to expect a conscientious, self-disciplined approach, always goal oriented, with an effective imagination. I enthusiastically recommend Albert as a person who shows intellectual promise, character, leadership, and creative intelligence. He is very deserving of this scholarship program.

Yours,

Michael A.N. Frei
Instructor of Biological Sciences

I did not get to where I am today without the help of others. However, I first needed to demonstrate the potential for a bright future. I needed to show that I could go places and accomplish things. This requires a survivor's mindset as opposed to one of victimization. If you find yourself in the latter camp, I need you to stop now and tell yourself you have already made it through the most challenging part—you ARE a survivor. You must not stand still no matter what life throws at you now. You must find a way forward, even if it is just one step at a time. It may be painful, but the fight must continue. The temptation to surrender may seem comforting, but you must search deep inside for that strength that got you this far. Tap into that energy and take a step. Close your eyes if you have to and take another. Leave your emotions out of it and push forward. A body at rest will remain at rest and be forgotten. Rest for us is to wallow in our sorrow. We must keep pushing on. Step after step, inertia can carry us forward as we leave the past behind.

To stand still is to concede defeat. You cannot let the world pass you by like a boulder sunken in a raging river channel buried in silt. All will have been for not. Did you survive the war to give up after victory? Accept that the world will never fully understand and make accommodations. It does not matter that life is unfair because the world does not care, but as a result, you are stronger. Just for a moment, set aside life's troubles. Cast away your fears, your worries, and your doubts. Imagine what you would love to do in life—anything. Move beyond basic sustenance and necessities like food, shelter, and safety. Let your mind wander. If you could do absolutely anything, what would it be? Now, envision yourself doing what you imagined, and hold tight to that picture. You can get there from here, and everything else will fall into place.

Understand that you possess a tenacity and drive that others may never realize. You have resiliency in you that most will never know. You finally have an opportunity to let your true self show. You are no longer fighting to survive but instead for your right to thrive. What is unfair is that you have strength beyond compare. You are no longer wasting all those efforts trying to protect yourself and can refocus your energy on improving yourself. Think about it: when your peers complain about their woes, how do those compare to what you endured? While others complained about their trivial slights, you were getting things done. For you, the war is won. Finally, living life is the spoils of victory, and you will not be denied. Time is too precious to waste, so you cannot squander it and wander about. When one has been where you have, they gain a heightened appreciation for where they can go. You have more focus, determination, and drive than most. You must harness these tools you possess for success and capitalize on them.

I did not know it then, but I was prepared for success and could choose any desired path. That was, however, until I received some news that turned my world upside down. I became that kid "most likely to be homeless" because I almost did not get a chance to graduate high school. The foster care system was pushing me out when I turned 18, months shy of graduating high school, because there was no funding. My foster placement[62] told me to move out the day I turned

---

[62] Years later, I had a chance to speak to my foster father. In hindsight, he realized I was nothing like my older foster brother, who had mental health concerns and got into frequent trouble with the law because of drugs and other

18 because the state would not pay any more; termination of child welfare services was to take effect on March 1st.

	CASE PLAN GOAL		
Name	Case Plan Goal	Projected Completion Date	Projected Date For Termination Of Child Welfare Services
Albert Grieve	Long Term Foster Care with Non-Relative	03/26/2001	03/01/2003

Adequacy And Continued Appropriateness Of The Case Plan:
Case plan is accurate and remains appropriate

The worst part is that I was not informed of this plan until my senior year of high school, and I was mistakenly engaged in school activities like newspaper and wrestling. Instead of focusing on school, I needed to be focused on life skills and seeking any employment I could find. Unfortunately, I had nowhere to go, no money saved, and no plans to bridge the gap between high school and college. I had no driver's license because my foster care agency did not want the liability. I had no immunization card or school records; I did not even have my birth certificate.

Whenever I address older youth in public speaking, I emphasize the importance of investing in yourself. If you do, others will invest with you.

---

things. After my foster brother was emancipated, my foster father allowed him to stay in the home—a decision that resulted in stress and financial loss. Despite my higher education goals and achievements in high school, he wanted me out as soon as the state money stopped. When we later spoke, I was thriving and grateful for the time he had shared his home. My drive came from the prospect of living on the streets, so I succeeded because of his decision.

But despite my school achievements, I had nowhere to stay until the start of any California university in the fall. I cut back on extracurriculars, got a job at Michael's, and enlisted in the Marines. Then I met Elizabeth Morrow from an HBCU in Jefferson City, Missouri. She promised to take care of me[63] when she learned what I had achieved and then learned about my background. She promised a full-ride scholarship at Lincoln University of Missouri, no roommate, and said I could wrestle on the LU wrestling team. Most importantly, she convinced my foster father to allow me to stay until I graduated high school, despite his reservations.

---

[63] I have had so much help along the way, empowering me to assist others without fear of condemnation or judgment. Without that help, I would not be where I am today or in a position to share my journey with others. However, I must reiterate that I had to help myself first.

Lorraine Gibbons   2-14-03
Families First

ALBERT GRIEVE

THE EMANCIPATION OF:

1. Albert turns 18 on March 1, 2003 that's only two more weeks from this date the 14th.

2. Albert will graduate from Laguna Creek High School in early June 2003.

3. Albert must locate transitional housing, a place for him to live by June 1, 2003. That's a must. A place he can move into the day after his graduation. I suspect he will receive assistance from Families First, the Independent Living Organization among others to accomplish this feat. I am of the assumption that Families First will play a major role the next 90 days helping Albert obtain housing, a job source of income, grants and scholarships, etc.

Let me know what I can do to assist.

John Thompson

Cc: CEO

Replace Independent Living Organization and Families First with Ms. Morrow and Lincoln University. Ms. Morrow one hundred percent lied about wrestling because the school had not had a team since the 1980s, but everything else proved accurate, and she has been family ever since. The day after I graduated high school, I was on a plane to Jefferson City with two UPS boxes to my name. I have never looked back—you can't. The same day I was featured in the Sacramento Bee,[64] and Ms.

---

[64] "It's about looking forward - College awaits bright teen who has seen - and overcome - a lot," June 5, 2003 Publication: The Sacramento Bee Page: B1 Word Count: 644; above the fold.

Morrow walked the newspaper into the sitting University President's office to show my scholarship was justified. I did not let her down. I was in student government, mentored and tutored, served as a resident student advisor, and graduated as valedictorian. I basically started life all over again.

I don't look at my past as a hardship. This type of adversity creates within survivors something unique to offer. We have a different perspective. We possess a difficult-to-acquire bank of knowledge. We also can connect with others and relate on a different level. After graduating from Lincoln, I joined the Jefferson City Police Department. While serving, I more aggressively pursued felony domestics than my peers. Since I walked in the shoes of people calling for help, I wanted to be there for them more deeply. I had a passion that the academy could not teach and a more profound means of relating while still wearing an officer's uniform. I asked different questions, ones you may not get from training but instead through the experience of walking in similar shoes.

As a not-too-subtle example, my father liked to lift me off the ground by my throat and strangle me. One of the things I remember is that when he would drop me afterward, I would be so dizzy and disoriented. Everything was spinning, and my lips would tingle because I was not breathing. When you are being strangled[65] you cannot move air. You cannot scream.

---

[65] Choking is an internal blockage such as food, whereas strangulation is external pressure on the neck preventing someone from breathing. There is a special prosecutor/co-

As a police officer, I once upset a lady while she was describing how an abuser assaulted and "choked" her. Concerning the strangulation, I asked if she tried to scream. Everything supported her account, but I needed additional facts to support the case. While officers can arrest with probable cause, I was looking toward evidence that would prove the case beyond[66] a reasonable doubt.

She cussed me out so severely but ultimately said she tried to scream but could not since she was choked. I submitted felony charges. Instead of merely putting a conclusion in my report, I was able to list specific facts and quotes to allow my audience to draw a conclusion which was more persuasive. The case still had to be proven in a court of law and I did not want someone merely kicking the can.

I had another "domestic," a not-in-progress call to a gas station to speak to the cashier. I do not recall if she had visible signs of injury, but I

---

trainer/mentor who would never forgive me if I failed to point out that distinction.

[66] I once had a charge packet refused by the prosecutor, meaning they would not pursue charges. After the briefing, my sergeant pulled me aside and inquired if he should go to the prosecutor's office. I only tried to send up meritorious charges, and it was abnormal for my packet to be refused. The refused packet was for shoplifting. The manager of a Conoco was reviewing surveillance video and noticed a cashier's boyfriend pocketed a lighter worth less than two dollars. The manager became very upset when I asked if she would accept two dollars from me and threatened to file a complaint. The boyfriend did not live in the county, and I admittedly submitted the weakest and most dispassionate charge code packet in my career, which the prosecutor refused six months later. Stealing is bad, but was this worth the resources to pursue?

remember she feared for her life and could not call from home. Furthermore, he (the abuser) knew the exact time she worked and got off shift, so she could not go to the police before or after work. These facts screamed to me extreme power and control. We arranged for someone to cover her shift for a few hours the next day, and I transported her to the police department. My sergeant had to make accommodation for me to do this because I was just a road cop who was supposed to cover a zone, which was incredibly exceptional considering I had little more than a gut feeling. The abuser was some little "insert expletive" of a man with a Napoleon complex, smaller in stature than the survivor. We gathered enough to submit felony charges, but I believe he ended up having his parole revoked. I could have responded to this call by giving her a pamphlet about domestic violence and suggesting she obtain an order[67] of protection. My past would not let me.

I have been able to tap into a passion resulting from years of abuse and trauma that drives me to do the impossible. This may be an understatement, but my life sucked. I do not wish my childhood on anyone; that simple idea has shaped my adult life. A few years after leaving the police department, I attended St. Louis University School of Law. I

---

[67] Get an order; but know it is merely a piece of paper until they violate it. The order gives the state more tools if there is a violation, but it does not protect someone from the actual violation. Some of the worse domestics I had included a violation of an order of protection. Take additional precautions, considering that getting an order served against an abuser may further anger them, and many do not care about the legal repercussions.

received the top grades in my Federal Criminal Prosecution and Criminal Justice Adjudication[68] courses. I had the opportunity to intern in the U.S. Attorney's Office, the Circuit Attorney's Office, and interned with a U.S. Magistrate Judge. After law school, I worked for the Division of Legal Services for the Missouri Department of Social Services before serving as the Legal Aspects Trainer for Missouri Children's Division. I presently co-train domestic violence with the Missouri Office of Prosecution Services and occasionally present at conferences while raising three amazing boys.

I fear no mountain. There is no obstacle I cannot overcome. There is nothing that can keep me down or hold me back. I know in my heart that anything is possible if I put my mind to it and work hard enough, propelled by a passion borne of hardship. With this mindset, I lead. I am demonstrating possibilities to my children, who already exceed anything I have done at that point in my life. As a survivors, our greatest superpower is the ability to break the cycle of abuse, neglect, and domestic violence, in a single generation—there is no kryptonite. I have done this because I refused to surrender to conditions beyond my control and consciously decided to help myself. Here is the catch (because we are always waiting for another shoe to drop): I have acknowledged there is a lot

---

[68] Law school was humbling. I was not the only valedictorian from college. Even more humbling was interning for a magistrate judge who obtained his law degree by taking night classes while working as an engineer at Boeing. He decimated my confidence in writing most constructively and with kindness, but I will always be grateful for his time and support. As you can see, I started writing again.

more work to do, and I am diligently studying my own trauma and the resulting impact to become a better version of myself. I cannot be the best dad or husband if I am unhealthy. You have likely heard you cannot pour from an empty cup; writing this book and sharing my story has helped me begin filling my cup. I hope I have helped others as well.

Chapter 12

Practitioner's Review

(prak-tish-uh-ner's ri-vyoo)

A practitioner has the power to save lives and change family trees.

As bad as my childhood experiences were, I am grateful that people finally connected the dots and saw the forest through the trees. A worse outcome could have prevailed. What took so long to see the big picture? There were breakdowns in the way the system should work at nearly every level that piled up for years. Every breakdown from individual investigations created future barriers and provided an inaccurate conclusion relied upon during subsequent encounters (especially when it came to my mother). It is incredible that the system ever got it right because of our trajectory and how difficult it was to course correct (reject the labels the system had placed on our family and see our situation from a different perspective). Claire could have been viewed just as my mother was and medicated as delusional instead of seen as a child reaching out for help when nobody seemed to be listening. The system placed Claire in a mental institution for her attempt to end her suffering by the only remaining solution she saw as a child. Ensuring this does not happen to others requires reviewing and learning from the system's failures.

Focusing narrowly on individual incidents, there was a failure to gather accurate facts reflecting events transpiring as my family members experienced them. Investigators could not look past the superficial lies[69] and dig deeper into what happened behind closed doors. A contributing factor could be that investigators felt uncomfortable challenging parents on their

---

[69] My father, post-incarceration, said investigators always accepted his statements at face value; never did they challenge his account.

accounts. How can someone help us if they are afraid of our parents too? It is difficult to pry into someone's private life while walking on eggshells. As children, we lied because we did not trust the authorities would keep us safe. This determination was made by each of us individually at an early age when the first encounter or two caused our situation at home to worsen. We were required to force the authorities to go away and avoid[70] drawing further attention. I was interviewed in my father's presence, so I did not feel comfortable telling anything other than what he wanted to hear me say. Even after interviews, I would update my father for fear that he may find out I spoke to somebody. See the following entry after my mother's death, but before we came into care.

Minor Albert was home, denied that he told father of my visit at school, then later volunteered that he had called his father from school immediately after the interview, but he only told him about the molest rumor.
Douglas Grieve presented as earnestly cooperative throughout the interview, but was evasive in answering direct questions and changed the subject quickly everytime the molest allegation was mentioned. He appeared to have difficulty sitting still.

"Minor Albert was home, denied that he told father of my visit at school, then later volunteered that he had called his father from school immediately after the interview, but he only told him about the molest rumor. Douglas Grieve presented as earnestly cooperative throughout the interview, but was evasive in answering direct questions and changed the subject quickly everytime the molest allegation was mentioned. He

---

[70] Visitation, once we came into care, delayed disclosure from me because I had regularly scheduled reminders (visits with my father) that reminded me to be careful what I said and made me believe my placement was temporary.

appeared to have difficulty sitting still."
(Source: California Department of Health and Human Services, Child Protective Services)

Generally speaking, perhaps the investigators could not dig deeper because they were so overwhelmed by their massive caseloads. They were trying to get in and out of my house, and therefore they were never genuinely present and thinking about the words as we spoke them beyond mere transcription for their documentation. They were not attuned to body language and did not assess whether the environment aligned with what we said or what one would expect for a household of five. Sometimes, investigations are like noticing a thread is out of place. It may be hard to see and subtle, but everything can unravel when you start pulling on the thread. Our home's cleanliness level was beyond abnormal for a household with children. Inquiring further would have demonstrated my father's OCD. That discovery would have colored his statements as being affected by mental health struggles; elevating statements made by others (our statements would get more weight because my father would be seen as someone who needed assistance rather than the savior). This could have led to a discussion of punishments for failing to meet OCD standards and, hopefully, his frequent intoxication. Instead, it was as if our statements were dictated to a transcriptionist. The significance was never explored when facts were accurately gathered, or troubling observations were made.

The result is the documentation I have shared, containing conclusions of each incident investigation that do not follow from the words they transcribed if the goal is to keep children safe. As you pan out to see the broader picture, gathered facts were not connected to the law, the law was not followed, or the situation was not viewed for the picture painted. Consider the hammer incident with my mother. The gathered facts agreed upon was that my father was swinging a deadly weapon at my mother (his wife) to place her in apprehension—to scare her into the home where she did not want to go—and in so doing, causing serious physical injury and disfigurement, requiring being transported to a hospital in an ambulance and receiving four stitches. No domestic violence charges were filed. In what jurisdiction do these facts not rise to the level of a crime? Why was the law ignored? What law states: "the following constitutes a felony offense unless it would mean children would be placed in foster care"?

If the impact on my mother's skull is to be ignored, what about the impact on the children in the household? Take the excerpt below regarding one of the many black eyes I received as a child and determine if the conclusion follows from the supporting facts.

9. **February 7, 1997**: A mandated school reporter reported that ALBERT was suspended the day before. Mr. Grieve called the reporter "a bitch" and "threw up his hands, didn't want him anymore." The next day, ALBERT had a black eye. The referral was unfounded. The child, ALBERT, denied abuse.

"February 7, 1997: A mandated school reporter reported that ALBERT was suspended the day before. Mr. Grieve called the reporter 'a bitch' and 'threw up his hands, didn't want him anymore.' The next day, ALBERT had a black eye. The referral was unfounded. The child, ALBERT, denied abuse." (Source: California Department of Health and Human Services, Child Protective Services)

The support appearing after the conclusion makes this appear to be a result-oriented investigation. "There was no abuse. See, Albert denied it." This may be another entry from the same incident.

"Possible physical abuse, 11 yrs. old seen with black eye, child stating sibling caused, denies abuse, other sib (15 yr. old) corroborates. Parents denied abuse. Children healthy, cared for. No evidence of abuse." (Source: California Department of Health and Human Services, Child Protective Services)

The following is from the hammer incident with my mother. Again, I am armchair quarterbacking to prevent these mistakes from happening to others. The term bizarre has not aged well.

"Emotional abuse – Fa. allegedly hit Mo. on the head with a hammer. Appears to be a bizarre accident. Children witnessed incident & were not disturbed by it. Family refuses any services." (Source: California Department of Health and Human Services, Child Protective Services)

What does it say if we children appear to have no emotional response? The answer is this was a typical occurrence. Children may not identify abuse between parents because they are told kids are punished to correct their behavior, so they may view domestic violence as one parent punishing the other. As to the severity, what happened to my mother was consistent with what happened to us as children. In other words, it was just another day. I have so many images in my mind of my mother lying naked on the bedroom floor as my father kicked her; what was one more episode? Maybe the instrument used in this particular violent encounter differed concerning my mother, but the violence was not abnormal, and the use of this instrument for violence had occurred previously. This was our normal life, of which the authorities caught a glimpse. However, it wasn't as much that we were not disturbed; instead, we became skilled at hiding how it affected us. To be sure, this was the incident preceding my first contemplation of suicide, because this life was so draining. I did not attempt suicide because I knew how bad my luck was (figuring I may live), but I met my lifelong road trip companion on this day, suicidal ideations.

Panning the camera out even further demonstrates a failure to review the history of incidents for our household and to talk to past investigators or others who interacted with us. Assuming high turnover, what could one determine from all the different calls, reports, comments, and inquiries? One isolated incident may be considered benign, but what about multiple? Consider a family you know well and unequivocally can say there is no abuse or neglect. Does that family have eight hotline calls and practitioners from different fields identifying red flags? Information was everywhere, but it had to be gathered.

12 Ms. Evans reported after the mother died, CLAIRE would call her father after every class. It
13 appeared to be that she "had" to do this. CLAIRE appeared to be driven to do this. Ms. Evans
14 reported after one of these phone calls, CLAIRE was rushing out of the office with a look of fear on
15 her face. Ms. Evans asked her if everything was okay. CLAIRE said, "Yes, I just have to get back
16 to class." Ms. Evans went into the office and was "almost knocked" over by the smell. CLAIRE
17 had thrown up in the waste basket and did not say anything. Ms. Evans was concerned that maybe
18 CLAIRE had reacted to something the father had said to her on the telephone.

"Ms. Evans reported after the mother died, CLAIRE would call her father after every class. It appeared to be that she 'had' to do this. CLAIRE appeared to be driven to do this. Ms. Evans reported after one of these phone calls, CLAIRE was rushing out of the office

160

with a look of fear on her face. Ms. Evans asked her if everything was okay. CLAIRE said, 'Yes, I just have to get back to class.' Ms. Evans went into the office and was 'almost knocked' over by the smell. CLAIRE had thrown up in the waste basket and did not say anything. Ms. Evans was concerned that maybe CLAIRE had reacted to something the father had said to her on the telephone." (Source: California Department of Health and Human Services, Child Protective Services)

At what point does the sheer volume of concerns cause pause and a deeper dive?

7 The landlord reported he did put a Voodoo doll, "well a doll", up on the door of the Grieve
8 apartment and reported another tenant had given him a doll that had "white trailer trash" written on
9 it. When he found the posters up in the laundry room, stating all he does is sleeps with his cat. He
said he put up posters stating that "Doug is a murderer, he killed his wife" and another poster stating
10 "Doug has unprotected sex with his stepdaughter. Someone please call C.P.S." He reported he put
11 these posters up but he believes that ALBERT may have taken them down before anyone saw them.

"The landlord reported he did put a Voodoo doll, 'well a doll', up on the door of the Grieve apartment and reported another tenant had given him a doll that had 'white trailer trash' written on it. When he found the posters up in the laundry room, stating all he does is sleeps with his cat. He said he put up posters stating that 'Doug is a murderer, he killed his wife' and another poster stating 'Doug has unprotected sex with his stepdaughter. Someone please call C.P.S.' He reported he put these posters up but he believes that ALBERT may have taken them down before anyone saw them." (Source: California Department of Health and Human Services, Child Protective Services)

I cannot explain away the DA declining criminal charges after the hammer incident. There was far too much documentation, concerns, and happenings to conclude the children and family were safe together (or remaining was not to our detriment). It should have never gotten that far, but to allow those conditions to persist afterward was appalling.

Isolation should not have just been a red flag, but instead, a flashing neon sign screaming, "We have no clue what's happening behind closed doors." Beyond just Child Protective Services, there were concerned phone calls from school, 911 hang-ups, EMS responses, emergency shelter visits, unusual statements to medical personnel, threats to shoot up the apartment complex, and other sources of information that were available. We were measurably isolated to hide the horrors transpiring at home, yet evidence of the atrocities seeped out. Extraordinary measures to conceal our activities alone is evidence. We lived in COVID-like isolation absent a pandemic—why? What was known was terrible, so there needed to be more extraordinary efforts to dig deeper. Too many sources of information existed which could have removed the belief that the hammer incident was bizarre and replaced that initial and unrefined thought with a more detailed and thorough panoramic view of what was transpiring. Then add to that perhaps statements from relatives, other individuals who interacted with us children in the academic[71] setting, and the neighbors who surrounded us where we lived. At the very least, the latter groups would have caused a trained individual who had the time to do their job as intended to seek more information and clarity.

Our childhood was a 2,500-piece puzzle, and the authorities were trying to surmise what the picture showed utilizing only a few pieces. In fairness, it takes time and resources to talk to other agencies, request records (sometimes requiring subpoenas), and interview neighbors and school officials. It is much easier and cheaper to get one collateral contact and move on to the next case. If something does not add up or if it does not make sense, label it as bizarre[72] and move on to the next case instead of putting in the resources required to resolve the unanswered questions.

Maybe the DA was too busy to see the hammer incident that had transpired just a few months before the homicide or the mountain of documentation from Child Protective Services. Maybe at the time, there were some political barriers that were preventing the DA from

---

[71] Educators should be provided more training (and compensated) on trauma, abuse, and domestic violence issues. If there is any doubt, look at the drop off in substantiated hotline calls when children are not in school. They play a vital role in keeping kids safe and healthy but would benefit from increased training. Since this entails a greater ask of this profession, it is only fair to ensure compensation commensurate with the services provided.

[72] What else could explain the DA citing as justification for declining to pursue homicide charges that they were unaware there was a history of domestic violence or child abuse?

cooperating with Child Protective Services, as unfortunately happens between agencies, getting in the way of keeping children safe. Maybe the hammer incident did not make it to the radar because no charges were filed, highlighting the importance of moving forward with charges and creating that record in case there are subsequent occurrences. I will not fault the DA for failing to see the domestic violence arrest that one Christmas, but I cannot help but ponder how a record of that arrest (since none can be found) could have changed future interactions with the system. Mistakes can and will happen. But when there is systematic failures of this magnitude, this frequently, irreparable harm and trauma is done.

*   *   *

I am often asked, "What can 'I' do?" The question comes from someone well-intentioned but with no exposure to the system or any idea where to begin. I believe those individuals can be the most important contributors. When I talk to others who are like-minded, have shared experiences, or work in the system, it is like I am preaching to the choir. Additionally, so many I have met in this field, like me, do this work to right the wrongs we experienced. So, we start the day already burdened by our own past trauma. Furthermore, due to existing systemic structures, we all know the struggles and shortcomings when helping others. Too often, we are forced to completely shut down from everything when we leave work and have little left to advocate during our off hours.

Even when we do, our audience is often the choir. Suppose people start to speak up who have not had these experiences, are not part of the system, are not dealing with secondary trauma, nor worn out and exhausted from trying to help others. In that case, those individuals can start to bring about change by showing that the greater society cares[73] about stopping domestic violence and child abuse, not just social workers.

The everyday person stepping up shows that combating failures to address mental health in our community is something the average citizen is passionate about, and we want our elected officials to address these issues instead of indifference and "lending a bat." In a perfect world, with enough people—average citizens—we could move our government and organizations who donate to charitable causes to focus more heavily on ensuring that entities that prevent and intervene in these social issues are sufficiently equipped to act before more harm occurs. In this way, the frontline workers will be in the moment and present during investigations because organizations can properly recruit, retain, and train their staff. Frontline staff will be able to dig deeper and gather more information with the opportunity to talk it over with peers if something seems bizarre. They can flush out the questions they have yet to answer to understand better what is transpiring and the best way to provide treatment resources or take

---

[73] The bar is set so low, just talking about these issues can make a substantial difference. Maybe we can start to infiltrate someone's social media feed who wants to make a difference. This can have a positive ripple effect.

necessary steps to prevent further harm. They could partner with other agencies, build relationships over time, and freely exchange information, allowing us to view cases from multiple perspectives without the hindrance of political barriers. Nothing prevents us from working toward this day except our failure to individually do our part. Let's dispense with excuses and slay every "no" until we find a "yes."

Until this day arrives, and even after, I thank those courageously fighting through these challenging cases steeped in mental anguish while exposing themselves to the knowledge of trauma to which humans, let alone children, should never be privy. Only through their perilous fight[74] can people like me go from surviving to thriving. This work is not a sprint; it is a series of marathons.

I have run numerous marathons, but none were more memorable than my second. My first marathon was cold and cloudy. I noticed people in all this legit-looking cold gear. I decided to attire myself similarly without considering the weather. I was dying, sweating profusely, and out of breath after my first mile. I still had 25.2 remaining and was unsure if I could continue. Step after step, mile after mile, hour after hour, I continued running. Do not get me wrong; the subsequent miles were

---

[74] I encourage other practitioners to share why they do this work to encourage others to join the fight. So often, when I present, I have law enforcement or social workers approach me on a break to acknowledge shared experiences. We must exit our comfort zone and speak out to demonstrate how prevalent these issues are. We need not continue to keep the abusers' secrets, and hopefully, others will be moved to help make an impact.

uneasy. Before I finished, I melted on city streets, seventy-one degrees under the open sun. I soldiered on so that the miles behind me were not traversed in vain; there would be a victory for enduring all that pain. My wife met me at mile sixteen with some more appropriate clothing, but I was already exhausted.

Nevertheless, I continued until I crossed the finish line. Completing a marathon is a tremendous accomplishment, so I was delighted, considering the circumstances. There was no fanfare or media interview, but I did it, and it was an incredible feeling of achievement. Similarly, getting a case right is exhaustingly but immeasurably rewarding. You may never see the impact you have, but crossing the finish line in a case like mine is saving lives and changing family trees. On behalf of those you have and will help, thank you!

The marathon serves as an appropriate analogy for survivors as well. One of the keys to my success in beating the statistics (i.e., not homeless, not perpetrating or incarcerated, not self-medicating through substance abuse, etc.) was looking past my childhood trauma. The effects of the trauma will always be there, but I can never wallow in my sorrow. I must keep moving forward, just like running a marathon. For survivors, it is like everyone else gets a head start, but we still have an *opportunity* to compete. Complaining about being disadvantaged changes nothing. Instead, we can turn our hardships into strengths.

Lying to investigators helped me learn the power of words and theatrics. Manipulation (persuasion) enabled me to become an attorney, and now a Guardian ad Litem representing children. Work-life drama pales in comparison to the atrocities I suffered during my childhood. I am in control and can choose when and how I will cross the finish line. Nobody can take away my achievements, and I have a greater appreciation for those achievements because I have had to work so much harder. For survivors like me, there is nothing more difficult than what we have already overcome, so there is no destination we cannot reach. My story is just beginning; what story will you write?

Chapter 13

A Weekend of Journaling

(a week-end uhv jur-nl-ing)

Trauma: "the gift that keeps on giving."

It doesn't matter what an outsider thinks about someone else's personal experiences with trauma and the resulting impact. All that matters is how that individual views and processes their personal trauma. Two individuals may have markedly different experiences that cause trauma. While we should not compare, for our purposes, say one person has an experience that is far worse. The person with the worse experience may deal with and process their trauma far better than the person we label as having an experience that is not as bad. As soon as we acknowledge that trauma is unique to each individual, we can start meeting people where they are.

This saying needs to change: "Suicide is a permanent solution to a temporary problem." I question whether whoever coined this phrase and those who repeat it have contemplated suicide based on severe trauma. The reason why I doubt this phrase is because trauma is not a temporary problem. Especially with children, it has been proven to have long-term effects on a developing brain, resulting in "trauma responses" to circumstances or stimuli. Even with babies, research is showing that the body keeps score. So, when someone relives their trauma through frequent invasive thoughts or vivid memories, how is that temporary? They are continuously re-traumatized through memory recall.

For someone to try to relate to my daily experience, I suggest reading this book cover to cover every month for as long as someone lives. Still, it is not quite the same, and they can always close the book. This book is my mind, and for me to close the book is far more permanent. Terminating the memories requires ending my ability to think, remember, or to recall. Suicide, for so many, is not an emotional decision. It is one arrived at by rational thought over an extended period of agony. It is a conclusion based on the facts they have, so to prevent suicide, they need to be able to accept new realities that change the calculus of their conclusion.

I think it is essential that we are not so quick to dismiss someone's rationalizations that lead them to contemplate suicide. If we accept their thought process instead of rejecting it, we can connect to them on a deeper level and hopefully have a conversation that provides other alternatives. If we dismiss them as wrong or crazy, we will never connect, and they will reject what we offer. Their conclusion was arguably based on limited facts (perhaps being isolated, manipulated, and controlled). By providing new facts, they may use the same calculus with those additional facts to reach a different conclusion—suicide is not the best option. They have every reason to quit, but maybe we can offer reasons to continue.

I first contemplated suicide at age thirteen, and suicidal ideations have been a lifelong companion ever since. When I'm in my darkest mood, suicide entices me with rest, peace, and serenity. Sometimes, I feel I was too weak to stop things as a child and I am too weak to end things as an adult. I tell myself it takes strength to fight through each day, but often those words ring hollow. Some bells cannot be "unrung."

Nobody faults that person running a marathon who stops in the race. I came across a statistic for the New York City Marathon showing that one percent did not finish, which is about five hundred people in a given race. Depression is like running the New York City Marathon mentally; it is equally exhausting and challenging to make it to the finish in any condition. As of information promulgating in 2023, suicide was the second leading cause of death for people aged 10-34. Yes, the second leading cause of death for children aged 10-17. "In 2020, suicide and nonfatal self-harm cost the nation over $500 billion in medical costs, work loss costs, value of statistical life, and quality of life costs."[75] So for those who argue against prevention and intervention, at least consider the financial cost (far too many do not value human lives or care about these issues until it impacts them directly).

It's ironic because attempted suicide also saved me, and in a way, I owe my life to suicide. Had Claire not attempted suicide after trying to kill my father, that 911 call never would have been made. We would have continued living in that environment, and who knows what would have happened, but I was struggling to put one foot in front of the other.

As an adult, I wake up every day often greeted by painful, wicked, and sick memories from my childhood. I did not create these memories; they were made for me. I go through each day hoping

---

[75] "Facts About Suicide." *Centers for Disease Control and Prevention*, May 2023, cdc.gov/suicide/facts/index.html.

memories do not resurface, or I struggle to relegate them to the back seat in my vehicle of life. With a little luck and a lot of effort, memories will share a backseat with suicidal ideations, which are always ready to take the steering wheel if I become too mentally exhausted. Thankfully, I have completed every marathon I have started. I'm still uncomfortable sharing all my struggles, but maybe this little bit will somehow help others.

Unless I learn to obliviate memories like Harry Potter or do a Vulcan Mind-Meld, I must struggle with re-traumatization through memories. Admittedly, I have not, in my knuckle-dragging ways, tried EMDR or other potential therapies, but in my defense, all of those modalities cost money. So, each day, those memories that fill this book are still there, and that saying ("suicide is a permanent solution to a temporary problem") fails to acknowledge or appreciate the daily struggle.

Instead, I must quietly try to suppress the thoughts, force them into the back seat, all the while they are cheering on suicidal ideations to take the steering wheel with its destructive ways. I get by, by trying to displace the bad thoughts with present positive experiences. I get the most positivity from my children, giving them everything and watching them enjoy life. I run, literally and metaphorically. I have lots of fish (fresh and saltwater), I garden, enjoy music, movies, and gaming, but it is at times barely enough. Nevertheless, I'm constantly pushing myself.

While writing this chapter, I was almost appointed to my first case as a Guardian ad Litem, but they realized the kid had been in care previously and appointed the same Guardian ad Litem. Yet another child is in and out of care in a system society neglects. I had mixed feelings about getting in the courtroom again, ultimately opting to push myself. When I litigated for Children's Division, I wanted to be perfect in every case because I know all too well the plight of each child, but the self-imposed stress was suffocating. I'm thinking about writing a book focusing on my healing. They say, "feel to heal," and I have felt quite a bit writing this book.

*   *   *

When writing some of the more difficult chapters, I tried journaling. The following are some excerpts from a weekend of journaling. I recommend journaling because whatever method used to write (paper, a typed document, etc.) has an infinite capacity to listen and is non-judgmental. I share these entries to let others know, who may have had similar thoughts, that they are not alone. I must also note that after this weekend of journaling, I took almost a month and a half off from writing until I could get into a better frame of mind. I have not attended therapy since it was mandated in foster care, but through writing this book, I have found a network of support to whom I can reach, although I probably would not.

Journal Entries:

> I was told journaling would be helpful. I'll try for a weekend. Today is Friday. I'll start with this. Sometimes, I just want to sleep. That's all. If

there was anything at all that I could do, I choose sleep.

> I am not advocating suicide. Seek help. I will, maybe...one day. But I am officially saying get help, don't do it. Feel free to ignore the rest of my ramblings.

> But nobody can really know, you know? I honestly believe that mother's trauma was misdiagnosed as psychosis. She was heavily drugged—hard drugs—that affected her. Her cries for help were always labeled delusions. Her actual death was filed as a tragedy resulting from a mental episode. So, NOBODY can truly know. You have to keep it in if you want to hold on to the life you managed to piece together. People say I am brave. I am supposed to say thank you. So, thank you. But it's a lie. I WILL NOT share everything. It will keep me company in my grave. I am not being vulnerable; I am still very guarded and must remain so. As a cop, I responded to a disturbance that was dispatched through a phone call, not over the radio. A lady jumped out of a moving car. It was at low speed, in a roundabout. No injuries. I thought she was fleeing. Her husband said it was a mental episode. He was a retired Highway Patrol and a reserve officer in my department. I transported her for a mental evaluation. We talked while she was in the back of the car on the way to St. Mary's. I know crazy. She wasn't crazy, she just needed to escape from her husband, but law enforcement was protecting him. I was part of the problem. I told her I really

understood, and I did, but I had a job to do. I'm just a patrol cop.

Back at the police department, I told a lieutenant (at the time) I didn't think she was crazy. I was immediately dressed down—aggressively. I was told he had more experience in his pinky than I had in my whole...something. I don't remember the last part. I got the jest. I was insubordinate for questioning the account of this reserve officer. I am no better. I needed the job. I didn't have anything to fall back on. No parental support. I dropped it—it became a heavy weight of guilt falling on my shoulders. I, more than anybody, knew better. I, in essence, didn't just hand an abuser a bat in the face of a pleading victim, I gave him my Glock and moved on to the next call. So no, I'm not brave, I'm selfish. But, sure, thank you.

➤ Some of the greatest literary works were not fully appreciated until after the death of the author.

If only there was a way to expedite the process... Then people may understand sooner... Just sayin'.

➤ Why am I complaining? I have tons of material things. Why do we value material wealth over mental health? It should be that way. Imagine the good Wall Street could do—could being the operative word. God knows I'm drowning in student loan debt to become an attorney in child welfare. What was I thinking? The quintessential example of financial illiteracy. I still don't feel I am educated and experienced enough for my

176

words to carry sufficient weight. I'll never be good enough, I'm trying.

➢ Sometimes, it is just hard to breathe. My chest feels heavy. I try to take deep breaths but still can't get enough air. I want to do something, anything, and nothing all at the same time. I want to sleep, but I can't. How do I make this go away?

➢ I sent a chapter to be reviewed by one of my acquaintances. I don't know if I really have friends. Well, I have a few, but I can do it all myself. It's fine. Why haven't they responded? It's bad. I can do better. I said too much. Maybe I didn't say enough. I felt so trashy the first time I tried to write about my sexual abuse. I can't purge that thought. How do you do that to your kid? I'm good. I've made it, but at times I am barely making it. Is this document secure?

➢ It was emotional whiplash going between the life I have now and the horrors of my past. I shouldn't say horrors, that is a conclusion, and it isn't persuasive. I need to prove why we are failing as a society—hold on, I have to change my son's diaper.

➢ My wife never has any excuses. She is very independent. We have been married forever, but I still must convince her we are in this together, and she can count on me. I have to be stronger than her. So, how do I tell her where my mind is and what I'm dealing with? Life goes on.

The physical abuse is fine; it wasn't me. Some other poor kid. How is my father having sex with my sister normal? I just told my middle son, "Don't look at my computer screen." I'm okay talking about the death of my mom. Am I okay? I feel bad I never told her that I love her. Well, I've said it in prayers. Does that count? People just don't get it...how can they unless they walk in my shoes? I was a pallbearer once. I wanted to decline, but how could I? My wife would never understand. He was an awesome guy that started mentoring me, like a father...I think. He was my second son's godfather and a family friend who died suddenly. There is no good reason for his death. His widowed wife needed help and support. I need to connect. What emotion do I use? Searching... searching... searching... I am a pallbearer and I can't hide. I must find an emotion to display. What is everybody else doing? That guy looks like he gets it. I'll copy him. How do I explain that I feel empty? It sucks that he isn't here anymore, but this happens. (I was there when my father killed my mother.) I usually just keep walking, but everyone is standing here, mourning. I just need this to be over. This is uncomfortable. I did it. I got through.

➢ It's been a week since I finished a chapter... I need to be more productive. Just saying, I'm a stay-at-home dad. What type of role model is that for my kids?

➢ People may get more out of reading these entries than my entire book...

➢ I may have moved jobs a lot because we changed homes so often. Apparently, more than I remember because I was so young for much of it. It really affects Claire. I also moved around in the system, which sucks. My father still hasn't shown up since he fled the place he was staying. Ashley went there and picked up all the belongings he left, including photos. This is the first time we have seen our grandmother, or who we think could be our grandmother. There is a picture of either his father or grandfather; we don't know. My father looks creepily like him, only younger like a little baby monster.

➤ It does not matter how I craft and organize the words that spring to life and dance on the pages in this book; readers with similar experiences will only fully comprehend and appreciate the deeper messages contained within the choreography of each sentence. Sure, I can get close, and I am trying, but close still falls short. It fails for this reason: a reader can close this book. The book doesn't follow the reader. Memories of something you read fade quicker and easier than those borne through experience. I guess you could read this book, word for word, every month for the rest of your life. But who would willingly do that? Besides, reading something does not invoke the same feelings, thoughts, memories, or regrets… Guilt. Vivid images replay repeatedly, and I remain stuck in a cell with them, unable to obtain a key to escape. Who would willingly remain without trying to escape? Well, I can escape. I, too, can close the book. But for me, it's a little more permanent.

➤ Sometimes, it is so hard to be present like actually engaged and sharing in the joy of unlocking a new epic. To be lost in damp caves of dark thoughts whilst trying to put on a happy face. I'm going for a run. Stress management.

- ➢ It was a good run, just slower than I wanted. It's hard to find time to run. Listening to music helps. Boost FM. I used to listen to Joy FM but I wanted something more upbeat, tempo-wise. I find myself running slowing with slow songs, if that makes sense. I really like NF. No offense to Eminem, but at least my kids can hear the lyrics.

- ➢ Claire pointed out the tree in my children's book, the father tree had a mustache. He also has a much lighter complexion than the mother tree, for tress that is—the subconscious is a funny thing.

- ➢ Life is a marathon. Just sucks not knowing what mile I am on. I'm tired...mentally. I'm fine. I have years before my oldest turns 18. I finish every marathon. I fight for that medal.

- ➢ I'm trying to put a story of love and hope (I know touchy-feely) out there for kids going through issues like me. I self-published Little One, You are LOVED. It sat for nine months online with basically no sales. So, I made it free. My middle son Kai read it aloud and I posted that video along with pictures and words. It's like pulling teeth to get some people to share it, and I'm competing with the likes of orphaned puppies and TikTok dance videos. So, I paid to promote it on several platforms, including META. This afternoon, I got an URGENT message that META suspended my advertising but they can't tell me why. Now, in the app, I see ads from third parties who I can pay to create an ad that won't get restricted. Seriously? I can't pay money to help others.

Then someone commented "F-off" on the children's book post. I feel like giving up, but I must keep at it.

➢ Life's hard. It's like a heavily carbonated beverage in a freezer. The bitter cold pressure is building, and it's hard to contain. Just gotta make it a little farther. I feel like I've almost checked all the boxes. Just gotta see my boys hit 18. Then I can release all the pressure. Then I can crumple my list and throw it all away. I can finally put my mind at ease. I can cross the finish line.

➢ Select all. Delete. Ctrl-Z. I live in the Show-Me state.

➢ This is not an expression of ideation. It's an attempt at a coping mechanism—expelling toxic thoughts. I don't know if it will work, but I'm trying. I think this is my purpose in life, the reason I endured hardships. To cry out for others. My mother tried to cry out. She was punished. Then she was killed, cremated, and forgotten. The DOJ records were destroyed a few years later. How do you like them apples? Have we progressed at all? I guess I'll find out. 37 Candles. Here's to hoping I don't get burned.

➢ It's Sunday. I think this is enough journaling.

➢ One more entry. Monday: yesterday wasn't a bad day, but it was "meh." Talking with some friends at the track helped. I think I can call them friends, but I always need to stay guarded. Yesterday was long, and that run took a lot out of me since I hadn't run for a while. I slept good. I feel good. META reinstated my ads and apologized for the "inconvenience." How could they know that could have been a last straw moment? I still don't know what I supposedly violated; how dare I spread hope to children! The conspiracy theorist in me would argue they were trying to drive business to third-party vendors, but I'll shrug it off. I'm going to make today a good day.

➢ Another final entry. Tuesday: yesterday, I took my kids to Bonkers in Columbia, Missouri, while my wife slept. She worked last night. Not my oldest; he was busy talking to a recruiter. He had a recruiter from Notre Dame and Duke call him the same week. I listened to his conversation. He told me he didn't want me to listen in to his conversation; it was like I was looking over his shoulder, but he gave a much more colorful analogy. If he only knew how much I understood (thinking about making Ramen with my father). He will be just fine. I did something right in life. We went to track practice. Watched a movie with my wife and started another before having to put the kids to bed. Today was a great day. Tomorrow will be, too.

What Readers Are Saying

This book relays a powerful message, emphasizing the resilience and strength of individuals who have faced heartbreak and abuse. Please remember that our experiences don't define us entirely, and people can overcome adversity to become survivors, parents, partners, and authors, as in Albert's case.

Jennifer Jenkins

Albert has laid bare a painful part of his childhood in hopes of helping others. I pray it helps both him and others. For someone with such a dark start in life, his successes and desires to aid others say a lot about this man I proudly call my friend.

Gene Parton

The story touched my heart. Albert is a man of resilience. Having been dealt a bad hand, he chose something more, better for himself. This is an invaluable resource for practitioners from a first-hand account.

Gloria Mays

Another resource by this author.

Little One struggles with emotions and difficult changes in life but ultimately learns how to move forward through a caring and nurturing environment. Follow Little One in learning the power of being loved and appreciated no matter what.

The author recommends this book.

A poetry book of a simple nature about a mother's love, strength, and demise from the perspective of a grieving daughter.

In times of pain or sorrow, poetry has been an outlet. Hopefully, you find something within these pages that resonates with you.

www.ingramcontent.com/pod-product-compliance
Lightning Source LLC
Chambersburg PA
CBHW061157120626
46546CB00005B/2099